Th

M000207355

'Those who know Blythe's earlier chronicles of parish life, *Word from Wormingford* and *Out of the Valley*, will find this one more directly connected with the liturgical year it loosely follows. But it has the same depth and breadth, variety and humour, tenderness and straightforwardness, with none of the lushness that often mars rural writing; and it is illustrated by exquisite etchings of country scenes by Robin Tanner, the Wiltshire artist who died in 1988.'

The Times Literary Supplement

'This is a book to be given to a friend who has a discriminating ear and an affection for things local. It is a book of our time.'

Home Words

'Using a simple outline from Advent to Advent, the book follows both new and old liturgies, expressed in the author's voice and enriched with his recollections, his delight in language and his passion for old churches.'

Methodist Recorder

'As a novelist, short-story writer, essayist and poet, the learned author naturally hails the Bible as the greatest work of literature. His very personal brand of theology has nothing whatsoever to do with smug dogma, sectarian bigotry or ranting cant — his low church leanings keeping a firm hold on ritual — but celebrates the beauty of words and the glory of creation.'

Eastern Daily Press

A Treasonable Growth
Immediate Possession
The Age of Illusion
William Hazlitt: Selected Writings
Akenfield
The View in Winter
Writing in a War
From the Headlands
The Short Stories of Ronald Blythe
Divine Landscapes
Private Words
Aldeburgh Anthology
Word from Wormingford
Going to Meet George
Talking about John Clare
First Friends
Out of the Valley

THE CIRCLING YEAR

*Perspectives
from a Country Parish*

RONALD BLYTHE

With Etchings by
ROBIN TANNER

THE CANTERBURY PRESS
NORWICH

First published in 2001 by The Canterbury Press Norwich
(a publishing imprint of Hymns Ancient & Modern Limited
a registered charity)
St. Mary's Works, St. Mary's Plain
Norwich, Norfolk, NR3 3BH

This paperback edition published 2001

British Library Cataloguing in Publication data

A catalogue record for this book is available
from the British Library

ISBN 1-85311-431-6

Designed by Vera Brice and typeset by
Rowland Phototypesetting Ltd, Bury St Edmunds, Suffolk
Printed and bound in Great Britain by Biddles Ltd
www.biddles.co.uk

For Jane Gardam

CONTENTS

INTRODUCTION

These are some of the addresses which I have read, rather than preached, at Matins and Evensong in three country churches on the Essex bank of the River Stour. They are Wormingford, which takes its name from the Saxon who lived by the ford; Mount Bures, so called because it possesses the fortified mount of a Norman castle; and Little Horkesley, which comes from *Hurk*, a shelter for lambs. St Andrew's, Wormingford, has a pre-Conquest tower and Victorian re-building whose confidence remains for all to see. St John the Baptist, Mount Bures, retains the kind of antiquity which penetrates restoration, and the feeling there is of great age standing up against constant wind, often making one sense that one is preaching on a sailing ship. St Peter and St Paul's, Little Horkesley, is a brave replacement of a fine medieval church which was turned to dust by a German landmine late one evening in September 1940. A Royal Air Force officer and his bride had been married in it that afternoon. The three parishes form the smallest united benefice in the Chelmsford diocese. Each retains a distinctive but elusive character which places a question mark after the word 'united'. However, they Christianly jog along with their differences and so far as I am concerned they tolerate the same words.

Although *The Circling Year* follows both the new and old liturgies, predominantly that of *The Book of Common Prayer*, it also follows various paths into literature and into the local countryside; so rather than set it out in strict order and thus reveal all kinds of omissions, I have made a simple outline from Advent to Advent, although not always with the official readings. A writer is a storyteller and here are my retellings of scripture. A writer is a 'voice', and here is my voice as it has been familiarly heard for a long time, bringing together as best I could my delight in language, my recollections of farming, my constant reading, my recognition of neighbours, and my hopes that what I have found in faith will be useful to the friends who so politely hear me out Sunday after Sunday.

Describing my own life-long passion for exploring old churches, I reminded those who shared it not to draw hollow, echoing conclusions as they opened an ancient door on to silence, for here is a huge arcaded room within whose walls everything has been said. Centuries of birth words, marriage words, death words, gossip, poetry, philosophy, rant, eloquence, learning, nonsense, the language taught by the hymnwriters and that of the Bible translators – all of it spoken in this place. A glance at the Incumbents' Board reveals that every old parish church witnessed (heard) the creation of both literary and spoken English as near a millennium of sermons battered away at varyingly listening ears. Thus each is a house of words, as well as the house of God or the architectural wonder-house of the guidebook. Being the local writer, it has been expected of me to add my own words to what has been said in church here for ages, and these are some of them.

The Cover Painting

Samuel Palmer's *Coming from Evening Church* has long been a favourite of mine. It is one of the works of the artist's 'night-self', as D. H. Lawrence put it, when he sees all human movement entering a visionary state. These Kentish villagers have been singing the Nunc Dimittis and possibly Thomas Ken's bedtime hymn. They stream quietly from church to their homes, soaked in prayer. At dawn their day-selves will be in the fields, vigorous, practical.

Palmer's congregation shows worshippers of all ages entranced by prayer. He once wrote, 'Blessed thoughts and visions haunt the stillness and twilight of the soul', adding that 'one of the great arts of life is the manufacturing of this stillness'. A friend of mine, the poet Charles Causley, gives a perfect description of this great picture.

> The heaven-reflecting, usual moon
> Scarred by thin branches, flows between
> The simple sky, its light half-gone,
> The evening hills of risen green.
> Safely below the mountain crest
> A little clench of sheep hold fast.
> The lean spire hovers like a mast
> Over its hulk of leaves and moss
> And those who, locked within a dream,
> Make between church and cot their way
> Beside the secret-springing stream
> That turns towards an unknown sea;
> And there is neither night nor day,
> Sorrow nor pain, eternally.

Charles Causley, *Collected Poems*

ROBIN TANNER

Robin Tanner (1904–1988) was an artist who created a link between the countryside of the Arts and Crafts Movement and that of the post-war years. He studied drawing and etching at Goldsmiths' College during the 1920s, became a Wiltshire schoolteacher and then an Inspector of Schools for Gloucestershire. He and his wife Heather Spackman lived with Quaker simplicity, saving a Jewish boy from the Holocaust and bringing him up as their son, giving away what they did not need, and following the ideals of Blake, Palmer and Morris. His etchings reveal the tumbling density of buildings and plants in rural England, an invasion of nature at all times of the year. As with Samuel Palmer, Tanner's work is entangled with ancient spiritual values and sacred metaphor.

R.B.

December: Elegy for the English Elm II

Advent

Ye servants of the Lord
Each for your Master wait.

Waiting, as we know, makes us fearful and apprehensive. The friend says easily enough, 'Wait for me at such a place and at such a time,' and he has only to be a few minutes late for anxiety and disappointment to overwhelm us. We wait for an appointment or an interview and sit in a row with those who are also waiting. We wait patiently at the check-out and in the communion queue. We wait to grow up. We wait for the best news and the worst news.

In Samuel Beckett's play two men sit famously on a park bench.

One says, 'Let's go.'

The other says, 'We can't.'

'Why not?'

'We're waiting for Godot.'

This person never turns up so the speakers never leave the spot, never do anything except wait. Mr Micawber waited philosophically for something, not someone, to turn up.

The prophet Micah said simply, 'I will wait for God my Saviour.' And this is what we have to do in Advent, wait for

God our Saviour. He will certainly arrive, though not as the fearful deity of the mountain-top but as a human child. Someone who will be both deity and one of us. How strange. How worrying as well as wonderful. Who names this child? An old poet calls him Adonaï, Root of Jesse, Lord of David's Key, Dayspring, Desire of Nations; and his mother, obediently, Jesus. It is not surprising that once a year we wait for him with as much trepidation as happiness. God is to become one of us to show us what we could be, what we should be.

The world was already very old when the child entered it, very old and stale and full of worn-out rules and rituals, and not at all full of love. Christ's purpose in being born into it was to restore the bond between the Father and his children, and to judge it for its cruelty, for its materialism and its ingratitude. We look forward to Christ's love but not at all to his severity. The pretty child in the manger is one thing, the Judge on his throne quite another. And so we wait in a confusion of joy and fear. No wonder the Advent hymns are so strange, so full of promises one verse, so filled with dread the next.

Advent is a thrilling season and a solemn season. If we remember that its name stems from the same root as 'adventure' we shall catch its drift. To set out on an adventure is both exciting and risky. Unsafe. Adventure means a hazardous enterprise. I once walked over Pentire, the great headland in north Cornwall, in the half-light of a December afternoon, and did not have to go very far before realizing that I was engaged in an adventure. Acres of plunging bracken and gorse, alarming cracks in the rocky earth, farm dogs barking like the hound of the Baskervilles, and the wild seas crashing many feet below. I felt unsafe, yet exhilarated, and this is how we are apt to feel in Advent. The air is filled with anticipation. There is hope as the promises of Old Testament prophets appear to be on the verge of fulfilment. All the longing for the Messiah is about to end. 'Come, thou long-expected Jesus,' we sing, 'born to set thy people free.'

Yet preparation has to be made. The birth of any child alters the home, alters the relationship between his parents, alters the world. How much more so must the birth of Christ alter everything which we have understood. Just before Advent begins we ask God to 'stir up' our wills. And the collect which we say throughout Advent – the most sublimely worded of all the collects – entreats God to 'give us grace that we may cast away the works of darkness, and put upon us the armour of light, now in the time of this mortal life, in which thy Son Jesus Christ came to visit us in great humility . . .'

However, the Gospel for Advent might at first sight appear to be out of seasonal context and more fitting for Holy Week. It describes the Lord's triumphant entry into Jerusalem. But soon we realize why it is where it is. 'Tell ye the daughters of Sion, "Behold, thy King cometh . . ."' *Our* King is about to arrive. So too does his herald, his small cousin John.

Hark, a herald voice is calling;
  'Christ is nigh', it seems to say;
Cast away the dreams of darkness,
  O ye children of the day!

The Christ-child's parents are lacking the usual arrangements and are in a muddle when he is due. They have gone to register at their native tax office during the last stages of pregnancy, less to obey the registration system than an old prophecy which said that the Messiah would be born in Bethlehem, 'the house of bread'. In Advent we travel the rough road taken by the Holy Family to the house of bread, ourselves ill-prepared for what is to happen, anxious yet happy, confused yet trusting. Eventually, we believe, all will be made plain. The blending of bread and love, our nourishment, is what we taste in Advent. It is the season of reverence – that reverence which the Bible calls 'fear', though not what we mean by fear. Call it a kind of loving awe. But what understandable awe when the local shepherds and the foreign potentates, country folk and great folk, arrive at the makeshift nursery and all kneel down – in awe. Mysteriously, it has happened at last. The shepherds sing – a song is all they have to give – and the kings give presents. I imagine them in some faraway bazaar: 'Have you something suitable for the Christ-child?'

A few weeks later, when the baby is taken up to the Temple for the ritual showing of another male to add to the nation's strength, two old people, Simeon and Anna, who have waited many years for this moment, know that they can now die in peace. Simeon cannot resist taking the boy in his arms. Thankfulness overwhelms him. 'Lord, now lettest thou thy servant depart in peace, according to thy word. For mine eyes have seen thy salvation.' He and Anna had waited for the Saviour. The shepherds and kings had waited on the Saviour. We await the Saviour.

We are very much on our own in Advent, which is less about the collective Church than about our response as individual Christians to the coming of Christ into our own particular world, and what we must do to accommodate him. Christ draws near to each one of us. 'Who draws near to God,' says St Paul, 'is one with God.' In Advent we personally draw near to a God who is no longer 'up there' on a mountain-top, but an approachable being. And not only this, but in the form of the most approachable being that any of us will meet on this earth – a new-born child. What an adventure for him! What an adventure for us! Where will it all lead? God ventures towards us, we venture towards him.

Alas for the delights of Advent, this gentle mutual approach between God and man is darkened by Isaiah who sees a Judge inexorably proceeding 'to argue his case and open an indictment against those who have "ravaged the vineyard"' – a quite terrifying figure. The great prophet is talking about the ruthless, often mindless, asset-stripping of our spiritual lives. Our riches are our souls, our tenderness, our sensitivity, a wealth which can so easily be torn from us by hard materialism. We must earn, of course, we must plan, we must be provident. There are mortgages, pensions, supermarkets, comforts, careers. All these things wait for our attention. But are we ravaging the vineyard? It is a question which Advent asks. Vineyards go to rack and ruin when all our energies are employed elsewhere.

> My beloved had a vineyard
> high up on a fertile hill-side.
> He trenched it and cleared it of stones
> and planted it with red vines;
> he built a watch-tower in the middle
> and then hewed out a winepress in it.
> He looked for it to yield grapes,
> but it yielded wild grapes . . .
>
> (Isaiah 5.1–2, NEB)

Something to Read

The international affair over Salman Rushdie's novel *The Satanic Verses* caused the great religions to take stock of their sacred texts. Many of their adherents had to ask themselves when they had last read them. The Bible was brand new for English Christians when Cranmer urged them on the second Sunday in Advent to 'read, mark, learn and inwardly digest' it – the Holy Bible, *the* holy book, albeit many books in a single cover. The word 'Koran' is Arabic for 'something to read', a delightful title which seems to conflict with the strictness of this book's contents. The Buddhists' oldest book is called *A Basket of Discourses*, which suggests a non-didactic faith. A discourse does not lay down the law but runs to and fro, offering all kinds of arguments and ideas. So the Buddhist mind is rather daringly free, not tied down but encouraged to range and rove. The Jews' holy book is *Talmud*, a Hebrew word for instruction. When we buy a car or a fridge or a mower or a wood-burning stove or a camera, an instruction book comes with it. *Talmud* is the instruction book which comes with each new life and stays with it from start to finish. My mother's worn instruction book, a ragged, much-used volume on the kitchen shelf, was

Enquire Within Upon Everything. Should you see a copy, however battered, on a jumble stall, buy it at once. Communists lived by *Das Kapital* – and how strange it is to put that in the past tense. Karl Marx wrote it in the British Museum for Germans and Western Europeans, not for Russians and Chinese. So all these how-to-live-your-life books over which millions have pored, and for which countless people have died, and about which endless other books have been written, have been seen as ultimate truths. They describe paths which have to be followed, and paths which have been abandoned.

I often think of the world's instruction books when I read St Paul. I recall what he wrote to the infant church at Corinth on the new subject of Christian conduct. You must remember that it was a church without a book. Did Paul believe that the letters which he sent to its various branches were all part of a new holy book? I think he did. Most converts hardly knew how to behave or what to think until they read them. Paul's sacred text arrived in scattered instalments but they soon came together, and the Church found itself with 'lessons'. The letters which contained these lessons and rules came to fine cities with theatres and libraries. They were lived in by a great mixture of citizens, Greeks, Jews, Romans, Arabs, who were accustomed to taking their spiritual instructions from poets, philosophers and dramatists, and who knew a good book when they saw one. So how astonishing it was to get Paul's book in instalments which said things like, 'as able ministers of the New Covenant you are not to stick to the letter of the law, but to that of the spirit, for the letter killeth, but the spirit giveth life'. Paul is reminding his Jewish readers of their first instructions on good conduct, the ten commandments. He calls them 'the ministry of condemnation', which is a sharp description of all those thou-shalt-nots. And he contrasts this stone book with that ministry of the spirit, or Christ's law.

Is St Paul telling these people, mainly Jews turned Christians, to abandon their old stone book? Not at all. He is recognizing the good and ancient law of Moses as the basis of all moral conduct, and not only for little Israel but for all the world. But, he adds, merely sticking to the letter of a law which says that you shall not kill, steal, fornicate, etc. is not enough. To purely obey the letter of the law is killing in itself, ignoring, as it does, all the possibilities of love. Paul then begins to set out a new covenant, a fresh instruction book on how to live by the Spirit. And he explains all this to the followers of Christ in Corinth, choosing this place well, for through it flowed business people of all races. This what he said:

> Are we beginning all over again to produce our credentials? Do we, like some people, need letters of introduction to you, or from you? No, you are all the letter we need, a letter written on our heart; any man can see it for what it is and read it for himself. And as for you, it is plain that you are a letter that has come

from Christ, given to us to deliver; a letter written not with ink but with the Spirit of the living God, written not on stone tablets but on the pages of the human heart.

(2 Corinthians 3.1–3, NEB)

There is a wonderful story of Jesus walking back from the coast near Tyre to Galilee, and having a deaf man brought to him. Mark adds that this man was not only deaf but had an impediment in his speech. How isolated he was in his silent world. Yet he had good friends because these had brought him to the great healer 'to put his hand upon him'. Christ did more than this. First he took the patient aside so that the ever-inquisitive mob should not watch what was about to happen. Then he put his fingers in the silent ears, after which he moistened these same fingers with his own saliva and touched the incoherent tongue. Then he looked up, sighed and said to the man, 'Ephaphatha' – be opened. It is what we say to the Bible and others say to the *Koran*, to *A Basket of Discourses*, to the *Talmud* – be opened. Show your heart to my heart.

Noel – and After

E very now and then a publisher has invited me to make
an anthology. I have in my time made a number of them
and can call myself an anthologist. The word comes from
anthos – Greek for flower. An anthology is a bunch of
flowers, chosen and arranged by an editor. The most celebrated anthology is *The Golden Treasury*, and my own
favourite, *The Oxford Book of English Verse*.

Well now, it has often occurred to me to make an
anthology of what children first heard in church – really
heard – and thus were able to remember when they grew up.
Some hymn, a particular prayer, some tale, a lesson which
flew from the lectern into their heads. The truth, however, is
that when we are young we hear very little in a specific sense
of what is said from the pulpit. Hymns and prayers are
different. So are Bible stories told to us at home and retold
in church. But *sermons*! I can genuinely say that I cannot
recall a single sentence which our rector, a Welshman, said
from the pulpit. And this is no criticism of his oratory or
scholarship, only a recognition of my own unreadiness for
the sermon. What I cannot forget is his swaying walk, his
heavy black bike propped against the churchyard railings,

his faintly bemused air, the loudness of his voice with its fluting cadence so unlike our Suffolk voices, and his way of saying our Christian names so that it increased their value.

One 'Sunday next after Christmas' Canon Hughes was away and who should be sitting in his stall but a very old bishop. A fat, long-retired bishop, as it happened, of enormous girth and stillness, dressed in crumpled robes. When the time came he rose and went to the pulpit and filled it. He carried no notes and, once fixed in the high oak octagon, he made no movement. Gaslight made his big face shine. His hands gripped the ledge, and the congregation and choir seemed to be waiting in a silence, which contrasted with all the Christmas singing, for him to begin. He then spoke his beautiful language into the great wool-church but with scarcely raising his voice. It was then that I listened to my first sermon. It was on the martyrdom of St Stephen. Ever since then I have pulled away the Boxing Day tinsel and holly, the mountains of wrapping paper and left-over turkey, to find – Stephen. The Irish do not say Boxing Day, they say St Stephen's Day. Some of us have our birthday on Christmas Day and get used to friends remembering it as an afterthought. St Stephen, St John the Evangelist and the Holy Innocents are the afterthoughts of Christmas, none of them going at all well with the decorations.

Stephen is one of the most charismatic figures of the New Testament and it is our loss if we let Christmas cover his face with its trash. To understand and appreciate him we have to

Christmas

know a little about the infant Church. Christ has died, has risen, has returned to the Father. Left behind are his teaching, his circle and his Spirit, which he called the Comforter. But what a world without him, that marvellous person who was so human though divine! And how frightened they all were at first. But now they have taken hold of themselves, these men and women of the early Church, some of whom were directly taught by him, and are beginning to teach others. As he said they must. Full of new courage, they have the nerve to teach in the Temple itself, where they were heard by all kinds of seekers of his kingdom. And not only did they teach, but they lived a strict communal Christian life, merging all their money and possessions. We do not have to be clever to see that very soon there would be all kinds of administrative difficulties. A religious community, however unworldly, has to eat, has to be clothed, has to educate its children, has to have homes, has to grow and make things. And so we have all that fascinating historic detail in St Luke's account of the Acts of the Apostles. There were many complaints, needless to add. One was about the distribution of food when the Greek-speaking widows were given less to eat than the Hebrew-speaking widows. The apostles then said that they could not neglect their preaching in order to wait at table. And so they chose seven men of good reputation 'to deal with these matters while we devote ourselves to prayer and the ministry of the word'.

It all sounds sensible enough but a mistake had been

made. We would call it putting a round peg into a square hole. It may have been his youthfulness which decided the apostles to make Stephen a food administrator when he was in fact a brilliant teacher. Stephen spoke Greek, the language of intellectuals. He was also a young man whose spirituality positively shone from him, so much so that, what with his personality and what with his sermons, he was in danger of getting the Church the kind of publicity which might alert the religious establishment to some heresy in its midst. We know the dramatic story. It is one which causes us to catch our breath. Unable to get the better of Stephen in ordinary debate, the Temple authorities arrested him. As he entered the court for his trial the Council stared at him for, as Luke says, 'his face appeared to them like the face of an angel'. Artists and poets have liked to interpret this as a description of Stephen's beauty. It means of course that he was seen in the courtroom as an accredited messenger sent from God.

Stephen's angelic authority did not stop the trial. By now he was the Church's first deacon and as such he was able to preach a sermon. Which he did. It is among the great sermons in scripture and it takes up the whole of Acts chapter seven. It reminded the Church where it came from and what it was at that moment. The court listened to it in awe. But when Stephen reached the point which revealed all too shockingly how Israel had treated a succession of inspired teachers sent to it by God, there was uproar. The scene was identical to that at Nazareth when Jesus made similar accusations and had narrowly escaped a lynching. Luke says that Stephen's charges 'touched them on the raw'. But by now the hostility of the court hardly seemed to matter to him. He was in another sphere altogether. He was with Christ – 'Look, there is a rift in the sky! I can see the Son of Man standing at God's right hand!'

It was all they needed. 'They made one rush at him,' says Luke, 'and flinging him out of the city, set about stoning him.' More follows in the shape of one of the devastating coincidences of history. The executioners, needing to put their coats where they would not be stolen whilst they threw stones, set someone who was watching to guard them. It was none other than the future St Paul. He was among those, says Acts chillingly, who approved of Stephen's murder.

This was the subject of the sermon which the old bishop preached to a boy many years ago, making an indelible impression of him. Had I been grown up I might have noticed how the rest of the congregation responded to it. But when you are twelve you can only see what happens to you.

Stephen stands for every young man or woman whose mouth is stopped by those who cannot bear the truth – except, of course, that his mouth could not be stopped. It continues to speak throughout the ages, through history, into suddenly attentive ears. As he lay dying in the stoning-pit, terribly injured, Stephen repeated what his Lord had said, 'Lay not this crime to their charge.' He knew as we do how often men are willing to have cruelty masquerading as justice. One only has to see Death Row in today's America. As for the coat-minder, the watcher of this horrible scene, his participation in it would very soon break his heart. It would make him in his own estimation 'the least of the Apostles'. Summing up his life he could only say, 'I am what I am', because he was rescued from what he was. Thus the new Church had from the very start its dark past. And Christmas itself, beginning so happily with the birth of Christ, runs almost at once into the murder of his contemporaries. The early hymnwriter Prudentius makes us stare hard at the futility of such acts:

> What profited this great offence?
> What use was Herod's violence?

At Candlemas

The Epiphany has always been an exciting time for those of us who, in midwinter, are only too aware of 'the frailty of our nature'. It goes straight to the heart, and to the imagination. It begins with learned men travelling towards a new light which has come into the world, and it ends with that same light being carried in the form of a child into the Temple at Jerusalem, itself the centre of the light-giver's own faith. Religion, of course, has its moments of darkness, of cloudiness, of obscurity. If it is ancient it will have rituals which are not as brightly understood as once they were. Such a fading of religion's true light was the theme of Amos's protest. Although not claiming to be a prophet, he said that he had a right to speak out against hollow religious practices. He was a young fruit-farmer and thus not the kind of person listened to by theologians, and we know what they must have felt about his ravings. All the same, it was upsetting to hear that 'the songs of the Temple shall be howlings . . .' And much worse.

In the cold of February we sing on the feast of the Presentation of Christ in the Temple one of the songs He would have known, Psalm 24. 'Lift up your heads, O ye gates, and be ye lift up, ye everlasting doors, and the King of glory shall come in. Who is the King of glory?' Why, this little boy being carried up the steps, as was every month-old child. The Eastern Orthodox Church knew this event as the Feast of the Meeting – the meeting of aged Simeon with his infant redeemer. For centuries in our country it was called the Purification. As with many mothers until comparatively recently, Mary went to a priest to be ritually declared 'clean' after giving birth, although this rite gradually became over-taken by gratitude to God for having given birth safely. To have a child was once a near-death experience for any woman.

We recall Luke's account of Mary and Joseph, in obedi-ence to the law of Moses, arriving at the Temple with the child. They also carried with them a pair of sacrificial doves, the symbol of love, for the altar. Nor are they likely to have been alone, for a constant procession of parents climbed Temple Hill to register their sons – possibly those same boys who would soon be massacred in an attempt to strike at the root of what might one day threaten a throne. The Temple itself was brand new, so beautiful that it moved the hearts of the Jewish nation. Herod had built it on the platform of Solomon's Temple, long gone. They called him Herod the Great because he had re-created Jerusalem, the City of God. But the little family arriving looks anything but great. Such ordinary people, a craftsman, his wife and their first child. In the shadows two old people are scanning every such group. They are Simeon and Anna, both in their eighties. The old man has read the prophecies of Malachi, a name which means 'my messenger'.

Malachi writes, 'And the Lord, whom ye seek, shall suddenly come to his Temple. But who may abide the day of his coming, and who shall stand when he appeareth?' – words made so familiar to us by the aria in Handel's *Messiah*. Well, Simeon abided the day of his coming, and so did Anna. Luke says that Simeon was waiting for the consolation of Israel and that he believed he would not die 'until he had seen the Lord Christ'. Had he been the usual kind of Messiah-seeker, instinct and a different form of hopefulness would have made him ignore this unremarkable trio. What, those people! Families such as theirs are ten a penny at the male-child counting time at the Temple. But Malachi the messenger's words now came with an urgency which Simeon had not known before. 'And the Lord, whom ye seek, shall suddenly come to his Temple!'

Simeon, the keeper of the divine fire, now took the light of the world in his arms, and said what we shall one day murmur, 'Lord, now lettest thou thy servant depart in peace, according to thy word. For mine eyes have seen thy salvation.'

After blessing Mary and Joseph, Simeon added some words which spelled trouble for them – for every one of us. 'This child is set for the fall and rising again of many in Israel' and 'a sword shall pierce through thy own soul also'.

Anna, eighty-four years old, watched. She had herself been married many years ago but for most of her life she had lived as a woman of prayer – she could be called the first Christian recluse, a kind of Mother Julian. Her role in this drama was to tell those who came to the Temple that the Messiah had arrived. She would have been a well-known figure, still and holy amidst the milling worshippers.

We have only one further glimpse of Christ before he grew up. All those thirty or so years about which we know nothing and about which we can only speculate. But all we have is the precocious twelve-year-old, back once more at the Temple, and daring to join in its intellectual debate. Daring too to seek an authority higher than that of his upbringing. This incident, so recognizable to every parent, allows us to see the normality of Jesus's life. It stops us from fantasy regarding those 'lost' years.

Candlemas, the Presentation of Christ in the Temple, is a day for those who are just entering the world and for those who are about to leave it. It reminds us of our innocency and our complex future, and of our departure. Scripture is filled with the passing of the years. It sets time against eternity, reminding us that our days here are finite and that our life in Christ is infinite. 'We are but of yesterday!' cries sad Job. Christ will not have this. 'You are of the present,' is what he teaches. 'Never mind yesterday, take no thought of the morrow.' Present yourselves in the present.

The New Year, like Jesus, is a month old. But we are not

babes in arms. We carry within us every kind of experience and, ideally, we should be mature. Our characters have been formed by what we have thought and done. The year itself will grow up, will grow old, and all in a dozen months. The spring flowers will come and go, the harvest will be combined; there will be one more May and one more December, and although the year will die, we may not, and probably nothing very much will happen to us, and the turbulence and brilliance of human activity will be confined to our television screens. But then, right at the beginning of the earthly life of Jesus and the start of yet another year for us, comes this illumination known as the Epiphany, this manifestation, this eye-opener, and caught within it that little group seen 'suddenly come to the Temple' to change everything.

> All thy Spirit promised,
> All the Father willed;
> Now these eyes behold it
> Perfectly fulfilled.

About Not Forgetting

The Church has a famous collection of statements called the Thirty-nine Articles which sum up its belief, but I don't think that they include a dogma entitled Memory. Memory is so personal and elusive that, although it is essential to a proper understanding of our faith, it can hardly be put into words which would suit everybody. There is a tender moment in St Paul's life when the great missionary apostle is paying his last visit to the little church he has founded in Ephesus. He has come to say goodbye to those who knew him so well, and who love him. And maybe this final meeting was too emotional for him to say what he had to say face to face. So he follows it up with a letter. It is a thank-you letter in some respects, but it is also a carefully constructed set of rules for the future. In it he tells his Ephesian friends to remember what they had been, and what they were now. 'Time was when you were dead in your sins and wickedness, time is that you are now alive in Christ.' In knowing what you are, never forget what you were. Remember that Christ brought you to life. Remember your former condition, how you once lived without hope, without God, and were so unhappy. And remember too that

I, Paul, am now a prisoner for the Lord's sake – and for your sake – and that I too have to remember who I was and that it is agonizing for me to do so. And yet I *must*.

Memory is inescapable and the years do not necessarily blur it. The young and the old are apt to have amazingly clear memories, although one of the diseases of old age can wipe memory out just as we can accidentally wipe everything from a tape. Our religious memory often includes things which our later religious ideas and practice can find rather embarrassing. Or persistently valuable and moving. I can remember a long framed text whose words I have forgotten but whose background set my fancies free, for it was a painting of ships on a lake – Galilee, of course – and my boy's imagination let them sail on to colourful ports all over the world. Even I could tell that as art this picture was terrible. Yet when in Wiston Church near here I first saw a masterpiece of medieval wall-painting in which a Galilean ship had journeyed in full sail for eight hundred years, it did not make me forget the boats travelling through the letters of that Sunday School text when I was seven. I *have* tried to forget the doggerel choruses of that period and find that they are not quite drowned out by the majestic hymns of school assemblies. Memory is a ragbag and a treasure-house.

I once went to Eastwood, the little colliery town where D. H. Lawrence was born, and there, a few steps from the miner's cottage which was his home, stood the dilapidated chapel where his family worshipped, then broken and derelict. Not a building to imprint some sacred glory on a child's imagination, as a Suffolk wool-church did mine. In this building David Lawrence had sung a chorus which went, 'Galilee, O Galilee, where Jesus walked in Galilee', and whilst he would soon reject Christianity itself, the word 'Galilee' hung around in his head for the rest of his life. There it was, magical, potent, long after religion itself had no meaning for him. I daresay that we all possess a similarly haunting phrase – one too 'simple' for us to mention as part of our spiritual awakening. Why hasn't our memory let it go as it has done so much else?

The scriptures advocate memory. They say, 'Do not forget!'

'Remember me when you enter your kingdom,' says the dying thief to the dying Jesus.

That instantaneous reply helped to shatter the loneliness of those neighbouring crosses. 'Today you will be with me in Paradise!' God and man perish together to live together.

A few hours earlier at a supper which commemorated his nation's deliverance long ago, Christ had commanded his followers, 'Do this in remembrance of me,' having changed the whole meaning of this feast in a way none of them could ever forget. Yet he himself, under the indescribable physical and mental pains of his execution, could at that moment only think God had forgotten him. Our own memory plays us false when we are under stress.

St Paul is insistent that we should not attempt to blot out

all memory of what we have done wrong. We can be forgiven for what we once did, or once were, but these are
among the hard facts of our lives. All the same, time will
take the edge off them. Paul suffered dreadfully from his
remembrance of Saul. The change of name did not prevent
horrible memories of what he once was from flooding up
and threatening to drown the person he had become. Nor
was it a private matter. All the apostles knew what he had
done. It was this torturing memory of his which enabled
Paul to come to grips with human nature at its best and at
its worst – and at its most complex. Also, he had a mind
which was trained to remember all kinds of things in great
detail – and in more than one language. For Paul there was
no escape from his memories, and his advice to us is, 'Don't
try it, you will only come to grief. Come to terms with what
you were before Christ made you fit for his friendship.' We
know that one of the roots of suffering is the attempt to
suppress memories. 'Don't,' advises Paul. 'Be mature, be
sorry, be ashamed, but be adult.'

It is the common experience to have running together
side by side religious conventions and personal religious
beliefs which are far from conventional, and it is the mixing
of the two which makes each one of us what we are. An
honest memory is the only asset we have which can show us
the self that God recognizes. It is the Epiphany when Christ
is shown to us in a full light and when we approach him
feeling rather exposed by the pure illumination of these

winter days. The collect asks God to look upon our infirmities – and how unhidable they are!

An Epiphany Gospel is about a different kind of showing. A leper, dreadful even so much as to glimpse, shows the Lord his filthy flesh and says, 'If you will you can make me clean.'

And Christ touches him and says, 'Be clean.' The one-time leper would never forget what he had been, so ill, so outcast. And in Christ's memory too there would have remained a sight of an unhealed and healed man.

A popular inscription for a sundial is, 'I tell only the sunny hours'. Being a sundial, this is all it can do. Given half a chance our memory would do the same, for it is human to seek oblivion for some of the happenings in our lives. But at the altar we remember our wickedness before we remember our goodness in Christ.

The Blacksmith and the Carpenter

⎯⎯⎯◆⎯⎯⎯

We all during our lifetimes make many things. We make meals and homes and fires and gardens. We make clothes and pictures and countless objects, some useful, some useless, and mostly without too much thought. God created us and we create recipes, flower-beds, shopping-lists, rooms and presents. Indeed there is hardly a day when we do not create something, even if it is too lowly to deserve such a grand name as creation.

In Isaiah 44 the prophet becomes worried about creation – where it can lead to. He takes two craftsmen, a blacksmith and a carpenter, to task. They are an essential part of any society and, as such, they might well lead us all astray. For as well as being artisans they are apt to be artists. Is the prophet against artists and only for artisans? Where lies the danger in the maker of useful things going on to become the maker of aesthetic things? Tables and chairs and horse-shoes and pots and pans, hinges and nails, yes, carved or hammered representations of the human form, no. But no to this easy definition of Isaiah's anxiety concerning

The Wicket Gate

blacksmiths and carpenters, for at the end of his book he prophesizes the rebuilding of Jerusalem and the Temple which, as later writers will tell us, would involve artisan and artist working together in harmony and inspiration. According to these historians Solomon's capital was the most beautiful city imaginable and Christians would use it as their image of the City of God.

So what is Isaiah getting at when he seems to restrict the carpenter and the blacksmith to their utilitarian trades alone? He is getting at idols, of course. The ancient Jews had made the enormous discovery that there was only one God. Surrounding them, and in all the far lands of the world, there were other gods, countless gods, gods for all purposes, and it was the artists' task to make each of them recogniz- able to the worshipper. The artists themselves ranged from the sublime creators of Greek statues to – and here was the danger – anyone who could use a chisel or a furnace. But the one and only true God of the Jews needed no such identifi- cation. They heard him say, 'I am the first and the last, and beside me there is no god.' He told Moses, 'Do not make graven images because if you do so you are bound to lend them some of my holiness (wholeness), and thus reverence them.' The use of any representation of human beings, animals and plants, whether carved or painted, was strictly forbidden by Jewish law.

And yet Moses had statues of the Cherubim placed on the mercy seat above the Ark, glorious works of art in beaten gold with spreading wings and looking into one another's faces. As for the furnishings of the tabernacle, only artists could have provided them. There is an exotic inventory of them in Exodus 25 onwards which makes the tabernacle sound like Tutankhamun's tomb. However, there is no mention of images in the New Testament other than the likes of those condemned by St Paul at Ephesus where he caused a riot by putting the silversmiths out of work. They had been doing a roaring trade out of making statues of Diana for the pilgrims to her shrine. Yet Christianity would be only a few years old when the first worshippers of Jesus would paint his life on the walls of the catacombs in Rome. Gradually pictures and statues and mosaics and representations of the Lord and his apostles would fill churches everywhere. Few could read so artists taught the gospel. Then printing brought widespread literacy; and then iconoclasts forgot what art had done in the promotion of the faith and for civilization itself, and set out to obey to the letter the ancient law against images. One meaning of 'iconoclasm' is to make a face unidentifiable. Thus we walk in cathedrals and parish churches alike to find many a faceless or headless saint, many a decapitated angel.

We now look at the little figure of St John the Baptist at Mount Bures or that of St Alban at Wormingford with affection but with no great sense of worshipping God through them, or of breaking the second commandment. And the anger we feel at seeing the iconoclasm of the Reformers is almost entirely that of witnessing the desecration of a work of art, not of encountering a holy person we can no longer put a name to.

That 'Thou shalt not make unto thyself any graven image' brings us back to the blacksmith and the carpenter whom Isaiah warned not to go beyond the practical requirements of their trades. Why? Because they possessed the skills *to* go further. Skills to make not only everyday objects but something sacred for the house. 'Is there a god beside me? Yea, there is no god. I know not any.' These are the words which the blacksmith and the carpenter should have had ringing in their heads when they fashioned something in human shape – perhaps, like the sculptor of the Angel of the North, in their own shape. Listen to Isaiah's fears:

> The smith with the tongs both worketh in the coals, and fashioneth it with hammers . . . The carpenter stretcheth out his rule; he marketh it out with a line; he fitteth it with planes, and he marketh it out with the compass, and maketh it after the figure of a man, according to the beauty of a man; that it may remain in the house.

(Isaiah 44.12–13, KJV)

But then the prophet takes the carpenter who has turned artist right back to being a man who simply cut down trees for firewood, but who even then was tempted to whittle away at a scrap of ash or oak until he had carved something worshipful, something saved from the stove and placed in his house. Isaiah is telling his people what a long way they have come since they used wood just to keep warm and to cook with. Making idols is primitive, something which people did before they knew that there was only one God. Yet we see primitive art on Easter Island or in the Lascaux caves and respect it. In fact it amazes us, and many artists try to return to it, finding it simple and good, so pure that God seems to have had a hand in it. Is it the hand of God in art which attracts our worship? Is the artist, the composer, the poet, like the saint, nearer to God than the rest of us?

What I love about Isaiah in this forty-fourth chapter is his tracing back of wood to its first usefulness and first appearance as artists' material. Man begins by being a forester, hewing down cedars, cypresses and oaks. He uses the wood to bake his roast then toasts himself by the blaze – 'Aha, I am warm, I have seen the fire.' He then carves away fancifully, as men are apt to after a cosy meal, is suddenly infatuated by what he has made and tells it, 'Deliver me, for thou art my god.'

Alas, says the prophet in his marvellous prose, 'He feedeth on ashes, a deceived heart hath turned him aside.' The forester who will in generations to come be the carpenter turned what is natural into what for him is supernatural, alas, alas!

Most of us are inclined to worship, not what we ourselves are able to make, but what we have the means to buy and set up in our houses. Our creativity lies in our having the skills to become better off and to surround ourselves with the best which the carpenter and the blacksmith can provide. The stern Old Testament prophets will not let us rest and are for ever pointing out the artefacts which detract us from seeing the one true possession, which is God. They, and the motives and drives by which we acquired them, are no new obstruction. In his hymn, 'O for a closer walk with God', William Cowper prayed:

> The dearest idol I have known,
>   Whate'er that idol be,
> Help me to tear it from thy throne,
>   And worship only thee.

Cowper was privileged and comfortably off. He was also a depressive. He had supportive friends. He knew fame and acknowledgement of his genius in his lifetime. We don't know what his 'dearest idol' was but it could have been his pleasure in this acknowledgement – so well deserved. But whatever it was it created a barrier between himself and his God. Mental illness too had set up a screen which at times prevented the nearness which he longed for. More than once in those black months he had attempted suicide. In that sad verse he might have been thinking of Isaiah's carpenter and blacksmith whose way to God was blocked by their own creativity. Like the deceived woodman, Cowper too knew what it was like to feed on ashes; yet like Isaiah he would often find himself in the divine presence and able to join in the prophet's happiness: 'Shout, ye lower parts of the earth: break forth into singing, ye mountains, O forest, and every tree therein . . .'

Daring to be Wise

When we read the Gospels we like to believe that they are dominated by love, and so they are. But they are also dominated by wisdom, something which meant so much to Jesus and which he urges us to seek. Wise men were at his birth, wise friends were with him during his ministry. His mother is reported as showing great wisdom, as ours were when we were immature and silly.

What is wisdom? Wisdom is the capacity to judge rightly when it comes to some important choice. Wisdom is soundness of judgement. Wisdom knows when to be practical. Wisdom knows when not to give advice. Wisdom can be a kind of balance of commonsense and imagination. Wisdom is certainly knowing when to go on and when to stop. Wisdom needs cultivation. People assume that they have it when they do not. As we look back we recognize unwise leaders, or are shown them on old footage, and we wonder how on earth they were elected. Unelected, unwise leaders are terrifying. The cry of nations over the generations is, 'Do not let fools arise to govern us!' But they did – and do. In youth unwise decisions are part of the process of becoming wise, and too much wisdom at twenty is unattractive.

In religious terms wisdom is a manifestation of the divine will. The founders of all the great religions are seen as sources of wisdom: the Buddha, Muhammad, Confucius, Moses, Jesus. Had their teachings lacked wisdom they would have been discarded long ago. The Lord ascribed all wisdom to God. All through our history wisdom has been given the highest place. The psalmist is absolutely clear about its origin: 'The fear of the Lord is the beginning of wisdom.' The beginning of wisdom? It is from this statement that we learn that we do not arrive at wisdom in one great leap but have to take many steps to it. Christians believe in their humble way that they do not begin to share some of God's wisdom because of God becoming one of us. The Bible shows us two kinds of wisdom, one up in the air, as it were, and far beyond the likes of us to reach it, but also down-to-earth wisdom. The wisdom of Jesus combined the two, the elevated and the homely. He said that it was wisdom to shut the door and pray in one's room, to be alone, to be quiet, to be contemplative. And that it was wisdom to do what was right and best whilst on earth. *Knowing* what is right and best is most wise.

All this, you will say, is elementary, and so it is. But look how muddled and unhappy so many people are because they feel that it is not their place to be wise – that wisdom can belong only to those from whom they have to get help. If only schools would give elementary lessons in wisdom.

Maybe they do. Life certainly does, but some of us do not attend its classes.

We have always admired wisdom so much that we encapsulate it in sayings and proverbs to remind us of undeniable truths. A stitch in time does save nine. George Herbert and his brother adored proverbs and made a huge collection of them during the early seventeenth century. Herbert noticed how his country parishioners lived by these little nuggets of wisdom.

'When a friend asks, there is no tomorrow.'
'Love and a cough cannot be hid.'
'It is a great victory that comes without blood.'
'Woe to him that reads but one book.'
'Of all smells, bread: of all tastes, salt.'
'Advise none to marry or to go to war.'

The Old Testament and its Apocrypha contain several books of 'Wisdom', among them the Book of Proverbs which Jesus would have known by heart. Job, Ecclesiastes and Ecclesiasticus, these are all wise writings, most of whose teachings are as applicable to us in the twenty-first century as they were to the old Jews during the reign of King Solomon. They are wise about work, falling in love, travel, staying at home, being ill, getting old, being young, marriage, ambition – everything which happens to us. But in the New Testament something quite different appears. We recognize it when we hear St Paul calling Christ 'the wisdom of God'. Although Jesus echoed the wisdom of his Jewish upbringing, he *spoke* a wisdom which had never been heard before. It challenged the traditional wisdom of his people, and it was because of this that their rulers tried to stop his voice. Yet he continued to quote from 'the wisdom of Solomon', reinterpreting sayings such as 'Wisdom is the breath of the power of God and a pure influence flowing from the glory of the Almighty'. When we read the wisdom books in the Bible we can see why wisdom was worshipped throughout the ancient world. Temples were built for the goddess of wisdom, Minerva.

Jesus took wisdom off her pedestal and returned her to the ordinary head and heart. Be wise, he told his followers. Be intelligent. Act properly. St Paul wrote, 'All the treasures of wisdom and knowledge are hidden in Christ.' It is up to us to find them. When the Bible speaks of things being 'hidden' it does not mean that we shall never see them but that they are there for the searching. We search Christ for his wisdom.

There are occasions when we have to make a wise choice, such as during local and national elections. Or when we have to fill a vacancy at the vicarage, or at the school. All set out before us are the candidates' qualifications for these jobs but they are unlikely to reveal whether or not they have wisdom. Reading them, I have sometimes wondered if it was wise for them to have applied! If we are lucky we might find in one of the references, 'We valued his/her wisdom on many questions.' One can have all the educational qualifications required for a position but if they are not accompanied by wisdom, then great difficulties lie ahead. The critics of Jesus were baffled by his teachings. They said, 'Whence hath this man this wisdom?' Meaning, perhaps, where did he get his education, this wandering scholar? He told them that the only qualification for entering his kingdom was to be like a child.

The last century possesses what no previous century has ever had – complete footage of its unparalleled evil – and as we watch the faces of those who imposed their ruthless politics on their nations we see, not so much cruelty as such, as an absence of wisdom. Hitler, Hess, Pol Pot, Stalin, the roaring crowds at the Nazi rallies, the Maoist mobs in China destroying their own culture, Mosley in the East End – the film is endless – all these individuals and actions are clearly unwise, stupid. Minerva has been deserted. So has all the wisdom of all the world's faiths, dumped by rulers who believed that it held back human progress. Wisdom has in its day been more gloriously enthroned and more often dethroned than any other virtue. It is the deep sanity of what Jesus taught which civilizes us.

> It was his royal ancestor Solomon who said: 'I myself am a mortal man, like to all, and when I was born I drew in the common air. When I prayed an understanding was given to me. I called upon God and the spirit of wisdom came to me, and I preferred her.

Wisdom is the brightness of the everlasting light, the unspotted mirror of the power of God, and the image of his goodness.

(Wisdom of Solomon 7.1, 3, 7–8, 26)

Septuagesima Spring

———◆———

In the current conservationist language I suppose it could be described as the time of the year when we 'ring' the environment. That now much-used word comes from the French 'to surround'. We are surrounded, or ringed, or contained, within those natural elements which make it possible for us to breathe, and thus to exist. Destroy or pervert them, divert them for some commercial profit, and we begin to die. This aspect of Septuagesima is too new for it to have a liturgical place in the Christian year. But from now on the Church can no more escape the environmental issue than can science. Or politics. Or any one of us.

There were centuries when Christians turned their backs on everything 'natural', from their own bodies to the earth itself, which they regarded as a vale of tears and the sooner departed from the better. Had they correctly understood the meaning of Septuagesima they would never have behaved like this. Had they thought for just one rational moment about Jesus's own feelings about being alive on the earth, they would not have behaved thus. When the Creator entered his creation it is clear from the Gospels that he delighted in it, and never for one moment behaved as if it was too 'earthy', as it were, for him. The teachings and actions of Jesus were filled with observation and reverence for his particular environment, urban and rural Palestine. His most loved village was Bethany, his favourite city Capernaum. In between stretched meadows, orchards, cornfields and vineyards. Not far off was the Mediterranean, the Jordan and the long lake where his friends fished. It was burning hot, it was very cold, it was wild, it was cultivated. He felt the sun and the rain, watched winter stirring into spring, saw stoniness and good soil.

The lessons for Septuagesima first describe in poetic form the creation of the world, then follow with St John's profound statement that before this creation existed, before there was physical light, there was present another light which he called 'the Word'. Thus the hymns which are set for Septuagesima connect our natural world with another universe, taking care to revere the physical creation.

> Lord of beauty, thine the splendour
> Shown in earth and sky and sea,
> Burning sun and moonlight tender,
> Hill and river, flower and tree.

When Joseph Addison wrote his creation hymn, 'The Spacious Firmament on High', it was believed that God's work was so harmonious that the heavens actually sang as they revolved. It was this music of the spheres which Gustav

Holst captured in his *Planets Suite*. Addison tells us, do not worry if this is not astronomically true:

> What though nor real voice nor sound
> Amid their radiant orbs be found;
> In reason's ear they all rejoice,
> And utter forth a glorious voice,
> For ever singing as they shine,
>   'The hand that made us is divine.'

We, if we like, can stick to that indisputable music for this time of the year – birdsong. Equally real is the flood of snowdrops by the churchyard fence, the catkins along my old track, the green corn running in the keen wind. Hardly a day passes without the Countryside Commission or the Green Alliance, or some stalwart defender of this faithful spring growth, urging us not to injure our environment, our natural surroundings, which include the seas. When the Septuagesima collect speaks of our being justly punished for our offences we know that they now include the destruction of forests and fish-stocks, huge evils for which in many small ways we may be to blame. The Epistle reminds in no uncertain language 'that every man that striveth for the mastery is temperate in all things'. We must no longer see ourselves as Lords of Nature but simply as a part of nature. St Francis did this ages ago. His *Canticle of the Sun* is a thankful recognition of the brotherhood and sisterhood of everything which grows, walks, flies, swims, warms, chills. And his 'Dear mother earth' is one great song of praise for its maker. He wrote it in his sunny garden, with early death approaching, looking for all he was worth at the loveliness surrounding him, and being so grateful for it.

The days are lengthening for us. Spring rarely waits for the twenty-first of March. We have only to go out of the old church door and into the village to see the actual springing. There is movement in the pastures, in the ditches. Live things thrust through dead things. The new and youthful Church finds its feet in the Septuagesima readings. On farms and in gardens it is work time. So we have the kingdom of heaven being like a householder who goes out early in the morning to hire labourers for a penny, whether they work all day or just an hour. And, in Mark, the rich young man who came 'running' to Christ, bursting out that he had kept all the commandments so what else did he have to do to be immortal? And we have a vision of 'a new heaven and a new earth' and a 'new Jerusalem'. What we in fact have at Septuagesima is the thinnest of boundaries between nature and other worlds than this. New lambs totter in the grass, new shoots depend upon the strength of old boughs, and our prayers speak of frailty and uncertainty, and that we should not put our trust in our strength alone. Septuage-sima speaks of the helping hand. We should glory in our infirmities – 'If I must glory, I will glory in them!' – because in doing so we shall be in the hands of God. That was St Paul speaking, of course.

When, in springtime, we read about people who lived all

those centuries ago, men like Paul, and the Lord himself, we realize how vulnerable they were to the roughness of nature. It challenges human self-sufficiency even now, with all our gadgets. But it also reminds us that at a time of growth we too must grow. Grow up! It should be good just to be alive. Thomas Traherne, a young man who lived on the Welsh borders in the seventeenth century, said, 'This visible world is wonderfully to be delighted in and highly to be esteemed because it is the theatre of God's righteous kingdom.' How Traherne adored the countryside, so much so that he once declared that he was tempted to do nothing except to lie under great trees and watch the clouds. Truth to say, he sat at a desk, like most writers, and worked very hard. Especially in February.

How to Give

———◆———

George Herbert notes how 'close, reserved and dark' we are when God asks for our heart. He came suddenly to mind because it was on Quinquagesima Sunday that his coffin was placed under the floor of his little church at Bemerton. The spring birds would have been singing in the rectory garden opposite. The Epistle for Quinquagesima, or fifty days to Easter, has St Paul looking through a glass darkly and speaking of tongues ceasing. Herbert understood:

> A man that looks on glasse,
> On it may stay his eye;
> Or, if he pleaseth, through it pass,
> And then the heav'n espie.

Both Epistle and Gospel for this Sunday before Lent are about giving – two very different kinds of giving. In the first St Paul writes about giving without love. Doing anything without love, he says, is worthless. He has seen showy philanthropists. 'Though I bestow all my goods to feed the poor, but without love, it profiteth me nothing.' He means that those who can afford to do so sometimes give in order to buy salvation. Such givers do not love the poor. In fact they dislike them the more for their having to be the kind of people who exist to give the wealthy the necessary leg-up towards honours and respect.

In today's Gospel Jesus gives a blind man sight, the thing which he wanted most in all the world. Jesus could have given him a kind word or a coin, which was what he usually received. But no, the great healer on his way to Calvary gave the blind man what no one else could give him – sight! He was ecstatic.

He had made such a din when he heard that the healer from Nazareth was passing his begging pitch just outside Jericho that he was told to be quiet, to hold his peace. But what peace could he hold in his state? Jesus forced him to say what it was he wanted from him. In as many words. A huge silence in which everyone heard the request. 'My sight.'

Then the giving of the gift. 'Receive your sight. Your faith in me makes it possible for you to do so.'

The blind man, now the seeing man, doesn't thank Jesus directly, but God, he who gave him the gift to give sight. The giver then walks in the direction of Jerusalem to give his life.

When Jesus told the rich young man to sell all he had and give the proceeds to the poor he was dealing with two kinds of hunger. The young man hungered for what we call 'a life'. 'Get a life!' we say. Jesus saw that the main impediment to this man's getting life in all its fullness was money. Alas, what he was told to give to receive such a life was too great a price to pay. So he went away sad. It was not as if he had not already invested heavily for this 'gift'. He had said his prayers and had remained virtuous, which should have been enough for anyone to acquire salvation. But Jesus sees a trapped soul, a young person already unable to move because of possessions. Someone who will spend what life he has looking after his money. Charles Dickens had him in mind when he created Jacob Marley who, you will recall, ended up as a ghost shackled with ledgers and safes so that he could hardly walk, let alone soar. Which is what we must do, if only occasionally – to be able sometimes to fly towards God. Today Jacob Marley would be dragging around computers and investments, mortgages and offshore profits, and a garage full of cars. Christ's anti-materialist law is a hard law for us – almost the hardest. It hits us cruelly below the money-belt.

The Gospels are crammed with every kind of giving, from the widow's mite to Christ's all, and all this giving would not be there if a tremendous purpose did not lie behind it. We know that one of the best gifts which is within our giving is not money but time. Friends and neighbours in want are often not saying, 'Spare us a pound', but, 'Spare us an hour, a day.' And we look at our watch or our diary and mumble something like, 'I could manage a visit on the twenty-fifth, about four, if it's fine.' Whereas Jesus is advising us, 'Give this person yourself for an unmeasured period and free yourself from your busyness at the same time.'

The blind man halted the healer by demanding mercy. Just before this exciting event on the Jericho road, that same road along which a Samaritan had shown mercy to someone of another faith, Christ and his little band had met after a solemn journey to Jerusalem to come to grips, as it were, with what must surely happen: that, in Luke's words, 'the Son of Man' would be spitefully treated and executed, but would rise from this dreadful death. 'But they understood none of these things.' They were beyond their vision. They could not see what he was getting at, this leader, sometimes as clear as daylight, sometimes as obscure as midnight, for whom they had given up their homes and jobs – everything. And so they walked on, as they had always done in his company, walked on and on, listening, half-grasping his words, and tired after seventeen miles when, as usual, the beggars at Jericho's gate set up their usual hullabaloo, one strangely insistent with his 'Have mercy'. George Herbert remembered to say thank you for the insights which God gave him:

> Thou that hast given so much to me,
> Give one thing more, a grateful heart.
> See thy beggar works on thee
>> By art.

The blind man would have 'worked on' many a traveller who came his way, else he would have starved. And they, the travellers, fed a mite more spiritually when they pressed a coin into his feeling palm. Facing the Gospel for Quinquagesima, or the last Sunday before Lent and its restrictions begin, we have St Paul's dazzling peroration on love.

So debased, so associated in our twenty-first-century minds has his 'charity' with hand-outs become, that we now say 'love'. To give without love, says Paul, is no gift at all. One of these days, he goes on, we shall see Love in all its glory, even if at this moment it is in shadows. And he winds up with brio, listing the best things in life – faith, hope and love.

When in *A Christmas Carol* the spirit accuses Scrooge of a lifetime of uncharitableness, he is bewildered. Has he not as a businessman in the City always contributed to charity? Who could not in his position? And we glimpse the ghastly world of Victorian charity in which 'love' would have been seen as something undesirable and rather a nuisance. For it would have awakened guilt and the glossed-over ethics of Christ. Today 'charity' is a postal matter and so professionally targeted at us that it often does not sound like love either. It appeals to our sense of values and to our common sense, to our generosity and to our hearts. The blind man appealed to the famous healer for all he was worth. He must not let this chance pass him by. A few minutes later he would never need to appeal again.

We may sometimes feel that the Lord was above money, like kings and queens, never handling it and letting his friends carry the bag. But the Gospels are filled with the ordinary economics of his day.

For example, the collector of the temple tax came up to Peter and asked, slyly, 'Does your master not pay temple tax?'

'He does,' was the answer.

Once Peter had the luck to find a silver coin in the mouth of one of his fish and was able to use it to pay the temple tax for both himself and his Lord. Jesus himself mentions money frequently though dispassionately. The Church's current preoccupation with it undoes his teachings on it, adjust them as we may, and our 'giving' is not what he meant by giving.

Paying the full price for what we have, this ever-giving faith of ours, is not demanded of us. On the right of the reredos in Wormingford church in the perpetual draught that causes the altar candle to waver, stands St Alban, a Roman-Briton Christian who got caught up in one of Diocletian's massacres. They beheaded him on Holmhurst Hill just above Verulamium about the year 209. The manner in which he gave his life had something in common with Dickens's Sydney Carton, who changed clothes with Evremonde in the prison and suffered in his stead at the guillotine. This is almost the most famous 'giving' story in fiction, with those celebrated last words – 'It is a far, far better thing that I do, than I have ever done; it is a far, far better rest that I go to, than I have ever known.' Alban changed clothes with a hunted priest, thus allowing him to escape Diocletian's soldiers and to continue to give Christ to those he met with along the way. King Offa gave us St Alban's Cathedral in his memory.

Quiet!

———◆———

In 1866 an Oxford undergraduate began a poem with the stunning line, 'Elected Silence, sing to me, and beat upon my whorlèd ear.' The poem itself was called *The Habit of Perfection* and was all about the call of the cloister. Choosing quietness can be, as Gerard Manley Hopkins reveals, a sensuous preferment even when it involves deprivations. We cannot have everything. Noise causes us to hear very little; silence makes us hear wonderful sounds.

'And when he had sent the multitudes away, he went up into a mountain apart to pray, and when the evening was come, he was there alone' – Matthew's account.

'And in the morning, rising up a great while before day, he went out, and departed into a solitary place, and there prayed' – Mark's account.

'Paul stood on the stairs and beckoned with his hand unto the people, and there was made a great silence' – Luke's account.

St John in his vision said that there was silence in heaven 'for about half an hour'.

As I consider these passages on a Lenten evening I would like to draw us into the precedence of silence. Neither Christ nor those followers of his who chose the desert route took it to silence the evil voices which they knew were in residence there; they took it in order to hear another voice overcome them. Deserts are ambiguous places. Their emptiness creates its own sounds, and what the poet called his 'whorlèd ear', like one of our ultra-sensitive electronic gadgets, often picks up terrible noises which the kindly bustle of ordinary life drowns out. The shape of his ear reminds him of one of those conch shells which he held to his head as a boy to listen to the waves of the sea, rising and falling, rising and falling. I tested this entrancing sound just before writing this, holding a big shell to my ear – and there it was, the unknown ocean on the unknown shore, falling and rising, and I too was a child again, and carried away by the wonder of it.

Writers usually seek a quiet life or at least a quiet room. I remember reading that when Thomas Hardy was working on *The Dynasts* in a room over the kitchen, his concentration would be broken by the cook and her friends playing ring-board below, laughing and chatting, and the great author would have to descend and say, 'Shush!'

We tend to forget what the loss of happy domestic sounds must have meant to Jesus when he elected silence. You may recall what precipitated his departure from the warmth and loquacity of a Jewish home to the cold wilderness. He had read the lesson in the synagogue. It was from Isaiah and began:

The spirit of the Lord is upon me, because he hath anointed me to preach the gospel to the poor; he hath sent me to heal the broken-hearted, to preach deliverance to the captives, and recovering of sight to the blind, to set at liberty them that are bruised, to preach the acceptable year of the Lord.

(Luke 4.18–19, KJV)

At first the congregation was ravished by his eloquence, then enraged by his criticism. They ran him out of town. It was the start of his homelessness. There he was, a young, wandering teacher and healer whose radicalism troubled the orthodox. After being baptized by his cousin John in the Jordan, he tested his vocation, as it were, by fasting for forty days. It was not an unusual thing to do. But for Jesus there was a special precedent. Moses had ascended wild Sinai for forty days and forty nights to receive the law and now he, the Christ, walked into the silence of the Galilean desert to prepare himself for the revolutionary restating of that same law. 'I have not come to destroy it, but to renew it.'

Our marvel is that Christ himself should have felt the need to prepare himself for ministry. But he did so and thus he elected silence. We can imagine that at first the Lord, like all desert listeners, heard exciting and encouraging 'voices' in this strange place where there were no human speakers. He might, like Gerard Manley Hopkins, have felt the blessed quiet of the cloister. But soon privation played havoc with the solitary Saviour and the tempter was saying, 'Come, have done with it. There are other, easier ways. Why be homeless? Why starve? Why put yourself through all this?'

Christ's answers are those for all our Lents and they break into our wordlessness. His people have always felt shocked to imitate him in his unique desert suffering, although George Herbert says, 'Have a go – he will understand.'

> It's true, we cannot reach Christ's fortieth day;
> Yet to go part of that religious way,
>   Is better than to rest;
> We cannot reach our Saviour's puritie;
> Yet we are bid, Be holy ev'n as he.
>   In both let's do our best.

Some time ago I walked Herbert's earthly way in Wilt-shire and now and then thought of deserts and silences. I wrote at the time, 'Deserts have been frequently seen as eco-logical errors which need correction. It is a view of them which would have puzzled the early Church, for which they existed as the ultimate places for hearing the voice of God. The desert flower might be the hardest to pluck but it was the prize of prizes. This flower thrived in silence and it was the special silence of the desert which drew men and women to it, not the hardships and inhospitalities of its location. These were mere travellers' hazards.'

Silence is ultimate prayer and those who sought it in the wilderness felt that they were breathing in and exhal-ing prayer. The Judaic and Christian faiths flowered from roots which had been struck in desert sand. Much of our

Christian sociability grew out of the Saviour's solitude. The Spanish poet St John of the Cross wrote of '*la soledad sonora*' – that vibrant voice which informs all solitudes.

> The generous heart upon its quest
> Will never falter, nor go slow,
> But pushes on, and scorns to rest,
> Wherever it's most hard to go.

In the Middle Ages cities were recognized as deserts, but deserts without silences. Bunyan called the city of Bedford 'the wilderness of this world'. Mother Julian's desert was Norwich but she got Christ to cultivate it. 'I saw a gardener digging and banking, toiling and sweating, turning and trenching the ground, watering the plants the while. And by keeping at this work he would make sweet streams to flow. The worth of this ground to the Master [God] depended upon his gardener's careful preparation of it. All around the Master was nothing but wilderness.'

In Lent we witness Jesus himself flowering where there was nothing but wilderness. The benefits which flow from solitude and silence are often the least-tried benefits and known only to the few. Kenneth Leech used to say that solitude and silence are necessary 'to preserve each one of us from superficial action, from exhaustion, from fanaticism ... Today the desert has come back to the city. It is in the city that we see marks of sterility, of dryness, of desperate isolation. Never has the city more urgently needed its contemplatives.' The countryside too.

That voice which broke into Jesus's interrogation of desert silence was all the more dreadful because it corrupted a beautiful text which he would have known. It debased the words of the psalmist when he said, 'For he shall give his angels charge over thee, to keep thee in all thy ways. They shall bear thee up in their hands lest thou dash thy foot against a stone.' Psalm 91.11 But Jesus would have also known the rest of the psalm which speaks of a very different kind of elevation. 'Because he hath set his love upon me, I will deliver him. I will set him on high because he has known my name.'

My favourite desert-dweller is Richard Rolle whose desert was the West Riding during the fourteenth century. He heard a singing, not a speaking, silence. He liked to sit on the doorstep and listen. He wrote:

> It is the tune that makes the song, not the words. The listener in the silence will be living in splendour and fire, and marvellous music will exalt him. He will pay no respect to anyone, even if they do think he is an oaf or a bumpkin, because in the depths of his being there is praise of God – and this jubilant song! For that sweet song is very special, and given only to the most special. It is not an affair of those cadences we listen to in church, nor does it blend much with the human voice, nor is it often heard by human ears. But among angel melodies it possesses its own acceptable harmony, and those lucky enough to hear it speak of it with wonder

and approval. I used to delight to sit alone, so that away from all the racket of life my song could flow more easily.

It has been said that Richard Rolle lived at a time when boys ran away to God as, later, they would run away to sea. Now and then Jesus too would hide away to hear the will of God – and there would be bliss as well as bitterness.

I Thirst

Jesus was intensely critical of aridity, whether in a person or in religion. He saw it as a kind of suffering. His heart went out to parched lives and dry as dust observances. For him, the desert was always within and he teaches us how to make it flower. He was full of praise for anyone who could bring refreshment to a parched soul. 'For truly, I tell you, whoever gives you a cup of water to drink because you bear the name of Christ will by no means lose his reward.' By this he must have meant common kindness, although some may interpret it differently. We know, when we see a friend going through one of those dried-up patches in life so common to us all, that it might be possible to offer refreshment, delicate gift though it is. Faith itself is frequently likened to a flower which needs watering.

Christ's favourite description of himself was as a well, a stream, a river. 'If anyone thirst, let him come to me and drink. He who believes in me, as the scripture has said, '"Out of his heart shall flow rivers of living water".' Assuaging spiritual thirst is a two-way business. That holy water-table which is Christ turns us into wells and pools by which others can rest and slake, perhaps, that terrible dryness which fills their days with dust. Each follower is asked to be a conduit for the river of God. Jesus said that there is only one thing we should thirst for – righteousness. We should have an appetite for what is true and good. Yet, being but human, we go sometimes for what we see as tastier stimulants, to find within us something horribly like the cracked surface of a spent reservoir. We are low. We could even be within sight of that most incommunicable of all illnesses, depression. We are suddenly struck by the meaninglessness of what was once all meaning to us. We are in severe drought.

Wherever Jesus walked he met with such drought of the spirit, such aridity in society, that there was nothing for it but to release the full flow of his love in both word and deed. A young man who had everything, as we would say, all the money he needed and more, a good background, a belief in God, nevertheless found himself existing in some kind of desert which was no life at all. 'How can I have *life*? Real life – eternal life?'

How does he come alive? Jesus saw what money and religious orthodoxy, between them, had done to this young questioner. They had dammed, and damned, the immortal flow. Alas, the solution was too drastic for the sufferer. It was, 'Give all you have to the poor – then *live*!'

He was no St Francis. The price to be paid for releasing the spring was more than he could pay, and so he went away sad. It seems a lot to us.

There is a little-known story about Moses which Jesus

may have recalled when he told the parable of the lost sheep. It comes from the apocryphal Exodus:

> While Moses was feeding the sheep of his father-in-law in the wilderness, a young kid ran away ... Moses followed it until it reached a ravine, where it found a well to drink from. When he rescued it he said, 'I did not know that you ran away because you were thirsty. But now you must be tired.' So he carried the kid back in his arms. Then God said to Moses, 'Because you have shown pity for this thirsty creature you shall lead *my* flock Israel.'

Like Jesus, Moses often saw his words as thirst-quenching: 'Give ear, O heavens, let me speak; let the earth hear the words I utter! My discourse come down as rain, my speech distil as the dew, like showers on young growth, like droplets on the grass.'

There are only two references to being parched in the King James Bible. One is said by Jeremiah when he compares godliness with ungodliness. Those whose trust is in God shall be 'like a tree planted by the water, and that spreadeth out her roots by the river, and shall not notice when the heat comes, but her leaves shall be green'. But he who has no such trust or hope 'will be like a heath in the desert, and shall not see when the good times come, but will inhabit the parched places of the wilderness'.

A Christian's duty is not only to seek that ever-flowing living water of Christ but to direct others to it. People are often parched through no fault of their own. Our responses to so many things which once refreshed us gradually dry up, usually without our noticing it. Time trickles by, and there comes a day when we say that life is not worth living – which can mean that we haven't enough life *to* live.

The second reference to 'parched' is in that sublime thirty-fifth chapter of Isaiah which George Herbert loved.

> The wilderness and the solitary place shall be glad for them; and the desert shall rejoice, and blossom as the rose. It shall blossom abundantly, and rejoice even with joy and singing ... And the parched ground shall become a pool, and the thirsty land springs of water ... And an highway shall be there ... and it shall be called The Way of Holiness ... the redeemed shall walk there: and the ransomed of the Lord shall return, and come to Zion with songs and everlasting joy upon their heads: they shall obtain joy and gladness, and sorrow and sighing shall flee away.
>
> (Isaiah 35.1–2, 7, 8, 9–10 KJV)

When Herbert became a priest towards the end of his short life he was given the prebend of a tumbledown church in Huntingdonshire as well as the living of two tumbledown churches in Wiltshire. Although poor, Herbert believed that it was his duty to rebuild the Huntingdon church, Leighton Bromswold, and there he did an enchanting thing. He translated Isaiah's holy highway into a wide aisle for the redeemed to walk in. Herbert's church at Leighton

Bromswold is in fact his poems turned into architecture. He was born in Lent, married in Lent, and he died in Lent, so he must have noticed that the chief dates in his existence were synonymous with the desert. Every great writer, every saint, knew what it was like to be dried up.

Contradictorily, some of the most refreshing water that ever was is to be discovered in deserts, both spiritually and minerally speaking. Water to lay physical and spiritual dust. Water enough to give away. Lent is for offering refreshment to others as well as seeking it for ourselves, especially if we know the way to the well. Christ shocked the Samaritan lady when he asked her, 'Draw some water for me.'

> The Shepherd sought his sheep,
>   The Father sought his child,
> They followed me over vale and hill,
>   Over deserts waste and wild;
>   They found me nigh to death,
>   Thirsty and faint and alone,
> They bound me with the bands of love
>   And carried me home.

Easter – the Password

One does not have to read far into Charles Dickens's *A Tale of Two Cities* before being gripped by one of the most thrilling passwords in fiction. It is 'Recalled to Life'. Even writing it down at this moment brings all my teenage excitement at reading his tale rushing back into my head. Set in the French Revolution, it opens with Mr Lorry of Tellson's Bank, Temple Bar in the process of getting an innocent prisoner out of the terrible Bastille. Very soon the Revolution will capture it and set free all its inmates, but only to fill it with other unfortunates, for this is what happens during revolutions. But first Dr Manette has to be Recalled to Life. This will be particularly difficult in his case because ill-treatment has driven him out of his mind. Thus his daughter Lucie, whom he has never seen, has to recall for him what and who he was before imprisonment destroyed his true self. Skilfully, unstressed, indeed unmentioned by Dickens, behind the rehabilitation of Dr Manette, with his emergence from tomb-like darkness into England's sunshine and Lucie's love, we are made to think of another dark tomb and from it one walking towards another woman who at first is unable to recognize the person she knew so well.

Christ's password too at this moment is 'Recalled to Life'.

Previously, in the sight and hearing of her and his other friends, he had recalled many a spiritually or physically dead person to life, reminding everyone what life *is*. His was a supreme understanding of the nature of life. He knew what a tragedy it was, for example, to be only half alive due to illness or loneliness or materialism, worry or strict obedience to certain religious rules. Some of those he recalled to life continued to carry the scars inflicted – usually self-inflicted – on them by their earlier half-lives, as we all do. But he gave them the strength to carry them. He was marked all over by what 'we' did to him here.

Here is one more Easter morning to add to the thousand which have been celebrated in our ancient church buildings, one more cry of 'Love is come again, like wheat that springeth green' to add to the alleluias of the ages. Christ recalls himself to life, so we sing the old Easter Anthems, high-pitched and ecstatic. They are the words which St Paul wrote with such certainty to the infant church which was finding its feet in Rome itself.

> . . . Christ being raised from the dead dieth no more; death hath no more dominion over him. For in that he died, he died unto sin once: but in that liveth, he liveth unto God. Likewise reckon ye also yourselves to be dead indeed unto sin, but alive unto God through Jesus Christ our Lord.
>
> (Romas 6.9–11, KJV)

Easter

St Paul would pull no punches. 'If you do not believe that Christ is risen, is recalled to life, and logically through him each one of you, then this new religion of ours is just that, a new religion, and all of us are being most foolish and to be pitied.'

The Resurrection is sometimes best believed when we remember how certain lesser factors have recalled us to life. Not necessarily those of the doctor or priest, whose task is to make us lively, but music, maybe, or larks on a spring day, or having to drop everything due to someone's urgent needs. Or it may be a new love or friendship, or just a new book. Certainly a new or awakened sense of gratitude. Jesus was constantly saying thank you to his Father. 'He took the cup and gave thanks', 'He took the five loaves and two fishes and gave thanks', and throughout the Gospels there runs a stream of unspoken gratitude, of thankfulness in his being *able* to do what his Father *wanted* him to do. All gratitude recalls us to life. Unconscious ingratitude – there is a lot of it about – denies us life. A basic tenet of Christianity is to recall others to life – not necessarily as evangels, for as St Paul wisely said, it is not for everybody to preach, but as intelligent people who can see some prison-house or other closing in on someone we know. It could be some neighbour or some stranger whose distress is obvious to us.

At this time of year it is impossible not to feel if only a fraction of that deathlessness which an Easter morning brings with it. On our way to church we see the low crops shining from the cold spring rains, see the green mist which precedes tree-leaf, notice the first flowers. The young teacher walking through Galilee used such resurgence to reveal his and our immortality. Consider the lilies, see this ear of corn, look at that vine, think of the sparrows, observe this little boy, for he possesses that simplicity which is the passport to my kingdom. Seeds were in fact his favourite symbol of resurrection and one that those listening to him, being country folk, at once understood. Easter Day is the feast of happiness and of gratitude in which we put aside everything which blunts our joy. On it, we are to think about the kindness of Christ. On it he forgave us, humanity at large, for the appalling things done to him on a beautiful earth. On Easter Day comes the warning that if we hurt or neglect our fellow human beings, we continue to hurt or neglect him. If only through the Church's ages we had recalled this reminder, then surely there would have existed now a far less terrible catalogue of our behaviour towards others. Politics is no excuse. Custom is no excuse. Military action is no excuse. Ignorance is particularly no excuse. Being 'sinners' is no excuse. Our ingratitude for all that Christ achieved is itself so great that we could hardly have blamed him for letting us make our way to his kingdom as best we can and *sans* those perfect instructions. 'What is man,' muses Job, 'that thou shouldest magnify him, and that thou shouldest set thine heart upon him? And that thou shouldest visit him every morning, and try him every moment?' How tempting it must have been for the Father to recall the Son from our incorrigible darkness to the source of all light, there to watch us stumble towards it with no clear path to tread.

A day or two ago, in a haze of pain, the dying Christ turned to a dying criminal to tell him that soon they would be sharing paradise, he, the perfect one, his companion in agony, the imperfect one. What was it that Jesus saw when he turned his fading gaze towards him? He saw a fellow creature made in his Father's image, thus recognizably his brother. What did he hear above the shouts from below? A few faint words of belief in the Kingdom. And thus the first person to believe that 'Jesus Christ is risen today' was neither disciple nor saint, but a convict.

We must not be surprised to find the reality of the Resurrection hard to understand – even to accept. Because so did all those nearest and dearest to Jesus, and there were soon a great many of them – 'a cloud of witnesses', the writer of Hebrews calls them. Throughout his ministry they buzzed around Jesus like bees, catching fragments of his message, clutching at his revolutionary ideas, getting themselves impregnated with his new law, that of love. To them, unlike us, he was not the King of Love but the teacher of love. 'Rabboni!' said Mary when she saw that he was not the gardener. Here was no royalty, only her old familiar friend – he who dragged her from her earlier existence and raised her up so that she could look him the face.

We believe that Christ's death invalidates death. He lives and so we live – 'therefore let us keep the feast'. Being Recalled to Life is a heady experience. We are not recalled to life for a lifetime in the earthly sense. The wonderful thing about Easter is that it lasts for ever. As poets are usually better than theologians at capturing this reality, let us hear Dylan Thomas:

> Where blue a flower may a flower no more
> Lift its head to the blows of the rain;
> Though they be mad and dead as nails,
> Heads of the characters hammer through daisies;
> Break in the sun till the sun breaks down,
> And death shall have no dominion.

Dylan Thomas, Collected Poems

The Frightened Walkers

In this meditation we come to the most entrancing of all sacred encounters, that which took place on the road to Emmaus. Scripture is full of journeys, long and short, and this seven-mile walk from Jerusalem to an outlying village in the country has printed itself on the Christian imagination. Two scared people slip away from the city after having seen all their hopes destroyed and come to nothing. Their main anxiety now is that they may have been seen as sympathetic to the person who has ended up on the scaffold. And so they plod on, their minds reeling from the horrors behind them and knowing that it could be their turn next. Heresy, blasphemy, being a public nuisance, these were great crimes.

It is Easter Day. The astonishing thing to us is that these disillusioned followers of the Master have disbelieved the Resurrection, because we hear them telling the stranger who has caught up with them, 'Some women of our company have astounded us; they went early to the tomb, but failed to find the body, and returned with a story that they had seen a vision of angels who told them that he was alive. So some of our people went to the tomb and found things just as the women had said, but him they did not see.' (Luke 24.22, NEB)

This is a strange admission. It would seem to state that although a number of both men and women had gone to the garden grave and found it empty, their evidence was not sufficiently convincing to stop the travellers on the Emmaus road from fleeing Jerusalem. Terror and self-preservation most likely came into it. But the women, the Marys, had not run away from the city, and as for that distinguished person Joseph of Arimathea, he had shown open allegiance to the crucified one by actually going to the Roman governor to ask permission to give him burial. What at this moment streams from the Emmaus story is despair and disappointment, terrible, terrible disappointment. It colours all the actions and responses of the frightened walkers. Also, we learn that they did not believe that their dead Master had come to liberate mankind but, as they said, 'to liberate Israel'. So it was a would-be national deliverer who had somehow let them down.

It was only at supper an hour or two later, when the mysterious fellow walker whom they had hospitably asked in blessed the meal, that 'their eyes were opened'. This was the second Holy Communion, the second Eucharist, or thanksgiving, of the Church, the celebrant being none other than its Founder. At this moment Jesus ceased to be their longed-for national leader and became the Christ. It was a tremendous realization, and a personal one. Just as he had at the beginning of his teaching refused to show his divinity by doing something spectacular, such as jumping from the Temple and landing without a scratch, so at the Resurrection there was no striding from Joseph's garden up to the Temple mount to amaze and convince the Passover crowd. Instead, he appeared to a scattering of those who had in their ordinary human confusion witnessed his divinity without knowing it. Mary Magdalen only realized this when he spoke her name, and the walkers on the Emmaus road when he broke their bread.

Luke tells this story. It does not appear in the other Gospels. It can be read, or interpreted, in many ways. It can be accepted as criticism. The Lord had reassured his friends over and over again that he would never leave them. An aspect of himself which he named 'the Comforter' would be present in the lives of all who loved him, then and for ever. But the walkers on the Emmaus road could not be further from comfort. They were perhaps what we might call Palm Sunday people, people who had been carried away with joy and expectation as that prophetically perfect claimant to Israel's throne rode through the ecstatic holiday mob. But neither God nor anything that this person himself could do prevented the ignominy which soon followed. Thus they were bitter.

When the stranger caught up with them, their faces were full of gloom, says Luke. And when he enquired what it was that had so upset them, they were short with him. 'Are you the only person from Jerusalem *not* to know?'

The fellow traveller asked, 'What do you mean?'

'Why,' they replied, 'all this about Jesus of Nazareth, that powerful speaker and man of action who we believed would liberate our country, but who our own leaders handed over to the jurisdiction of the occupying power for trial and execution!' Meaning that one could hardly have missed such an event. It rocked the town.

It was then that they admitted their own faithlessness. 'Some women of our company have astounded us: they went early to the tomb this morning and failed to find his body . . .' They were neither cheered nor bewildered by this account. Nor had they gone to the tomb themselves to find out if it was true. They had simply and sadly tramped home. What, we might ask, had they been doing in Jerusalem all day? The women had gone to the tomb at break of day and now it was late evening. It was about seven miles from the city to their village, about a two-hour walk. Probably they had lain low until it began to get dark, scared of being picked up by the police.

As all three now stepped it out, the stranger chided his companions for being so dull. It was a word they would often have heard from the Master who often complained that his friends were thick-headed. He adored simplicity, was forgiving when it came to plain ignorance, but had no patience with dullness. 'How dull you are!' He then gave them a history lesson on the prophetic scriptures. Still they did not recognize him.

At last they reached Emmaus – this is the only reference

to this place in the Bible but no village would carry with it such an electric association. The talkative stranger made as if to walk on, and then came the exquisite invitation, 'Abide with us, for it is toward evening and the day is far spent.' Henry Lyte would open his great hymn with those words: 'Abide with me, fast falls the eventide.' They are the first words of the post-Resurrection world beseeching Christ to enter it as a guest. The walkers would have known an old injunction which said that those who entertain strangers sometimes entertain angels unawares. Anyway, we know that 'he went in to tarry with them' and then at supper 'he took bread and blessed it, and brake it and gave it to them'.

Now they knew! Now they could see who it was. Now the dullness fled, as did all the fear. Now they saw only too clearly as 'he vanished out of their sight'. Did they go to bed, worn out but happy? No, they set off back to Jerusalem that very same hour, strong, confident, refreshed, nourished. They found the Eleven and as they were pouring out their tale, the risen Jesus appeared in their midst, first terrifying them, then bringing them that peace which is beyond human understanding.

The Emmaus Road Christ has become every Christian's intimate Jesus. The faith would now always be seen as a journey, sometimes easy enough, then rough, a place of pitfalls and sudden glorious views, of miles and miles of loneliness and delightful encounters, of dangers and exhaustion. We dread the ending of the road, no matter how rough it may be.

But always there is the one who keeps step with us, who knew what tiredness was.

Luke's story ends in another village, this one only a mile or two from the city – Bethany. It was there during his human experience that the homeless Jesus was welcome at any time and where a brother and his sisters welcomed him in. It was from there, too, says Luke, that he led his followers out, and as he lifted up his hands to bless them, he parted from them to be with his Father.

There is a tremendous clamour about Holy Week, with its noisy processions, law courts, torture, rabble shouts and holiday hubbub. Then comes the most ordinary event, the quiet walk back home.

Keeping Up with Mark

The four Gospels are stylistically most distinctive even if they must necessarily be much the same in content. The good news was the same good news whoever wrote it down in order that it could be carried, not by word of mouth, for this would have soon distorted it, but in Greek writing. All the most respected thought of the ancient world was put into Greek. The sublimely simple words of Jesus, though spoken in his native Aramaic, were made intellectually respectable when heard in Greek.

It is bright, clear late April, the time of the author of the second Gospel, Mark. Who was Mark? And why is his Gospel so thrillingly readable? And to whom was it addressed? There are writers who address themselves to an individual or to a particular readership, but Mark addresses the universe. His Greek is not the grand language of scholarship but the kind of common Greek by means of which all kinds of people made themselves understood in the many-tongued Mediterranean. The Lord's tongue and the Latin tongue show through Mark's rough Greek with powerful effect. How intimately close we are to his Master when we read Mark. They called him an Evangel, a proclaimer of good news, and because of the hurry and urgency of his proclamation he has become the Ezekiel of the New Testament. His lion symbol is borrowed from Ezekiel's winged lion, the noise of whose wings was like a great torrent or cloudburst, or like that of an armed camp, or a multitude. Lions roar. Ezekiel is not a gentle prophet. He is young and turbulent, full of eagerness, full of warning. He said, 'A spirit lifted me and carried me along, and I went full of exaltation, the hand of the Lord strong upon me.'

Mark too is lifted by the Spirit. He is a winged intellect but one who can be popularly understood. His Gospel moves at a tremendous pace. It is the shortest of the four books of Christ and it carries the reader along at breakneck speed. Mark, like all good authors, knows how to keep the pages turning. In his book there is no birth of the Saviour, no growing up of the precocious holy boy. It opens with the Baptist's herald-cry 'Prepare a way for the Lord!' The temptation in the wilderness takes Mark about twenty-five words to describe and then all the rest of the divine story follows fast. It is significant that only in Mark do we have the parable of the sower and the parable about keeping awake. Mark is a broadcaster – a description, which comes from the casting of seed over the fields in springtime. He knows all about waste and inattention, and about his words being swallowed up by short-lived cults, or falling where they cannot possibly take. He knew too that here and there they would survive, would grow, would change the world. This particular story told by Jesus would have had a special attraction for him. He tells it perfectly and so it has become, over the centuries, one of the most loved and most trusted of all the Gospel tales.

But the 'Keep awake' parable, for all Mark's art, remains little known, perhaps because it is so brief. Here it is:

> Be alert, be wakeful. You do not know when the moment comes. It is like a man away from home: he has left his house and put his servants in charge, each with his own work to do, and he has ordered the door-keeper to stay awake. *Keep awake*, then, for you do not know when the master of the house is coming. Evening or midnight, cock-crow or early dawn – if he comes suddenly, he must not find you asleep. And what I say to you I say to everyone: Keep awake.

(Mark 13.33–7, NEB)

Not that there is much likelihood of dozing with Mark around. He doesn't write to soothe, he writes to activate. He restates the teachings of Jesus with a commanding forceful-ness. His prose is swift and certain. There is no hanging about, no decoration. Mark's Gospel is the message made plain as a pikestaff and clear-running as a brook.

Who was Mark? Well, as the cousin of Barnabas he may have been a Cypriot. We first encounter him when Peter takes shelter in Mark's mother's house in Jerusalem after escaping from prison, and Peter it must have been who con-verted him. And Paul it was who took him along with him on those epic missionary journeys. Paul too had Romanized his Jewish name. Paul too had been commissioned by Christ to carry his teachings to all the world, and not leave them as a renewal of the old laws of the Jews in Palestine. Thus Mark's credentials could not be more impressive, converted by Peter the Rock of the new Church, made an evangel by Paul its proto-missionary. Mark ends his wonderful Gospel with these words: 'Afterwards Jesus himself sent out by them from east to west the sacred and imperishable message of eternal salvation.' These were among Mark's last written words. Their abruptness suggests that there may have been more which have become lost.

Mark, like Ezekiel's dream-lion with its rolling eyes and soaring wings, might have been too symbolic a creature had we not been given one of the most tenderly human accounts of an evangel to be found in scripture in Paul's Letter to Timothy. Paul is old and battered and facing death, and so he sits down to write fatherly letters to the youthful ministers who must succeed him. He writes one letter to Titus and two to Timothy, whom he calls 'my dear son'. He tells Timothy that he, Paul, is herald, apostle and teacher of the Gospel, and now that he is handing over these great roles Timothy must 'turn from the wayward impulses of youth and pursue integrity, love and peace'. 'You, my dear son, have followed, step by step, my teaching and my manner of life', for now 'I have run the great race, have finished the course, and the prize awaits me.' Paul adds, 'Do your best to join me soon – I have no one with me but Luke . . . *Pick up Mark and bring him with you, for I find him a useful assistant* . . . When you come, bring the cloak I left with Carpus, and the books, above all my notebooks.' Imagine fetching St Paul his cloak and notebooks and picking up St Mark on the way! It is intimate detail such as this which de-mists time.

They say that Mark went on to Christianize Egypt and was murdered there. But this is apocryphal. What is certain is that a literary master who could be understood by the masses wrote his version of the Gospel in a style whose brevity, beauty and swiftness can still leave us breathless. As Laurence Housman said,

> And so may all whose minds are dark
> Be led to truth by good Saint Mark.

Another poet, John Keats, wrote *The Eve of Saint Mark*. Like the lion-apostle's Gospel, it remains unfinished. It contains a coldly accurate description of England at St Mark's-tide:

> The city streets were clean and fair
> From wholesome drench of April rains;
> And, on the western window panes,
> The chilly sunset faintly told
> Of unmatured vallies cold,
> Of the green thorny bloomless hedge,
> Of rivers new with spring-tide sedge,
> Of primroses by shelter'd rills,
> And daisies on the aguish hills.

In the poem a girl closes an illuminated old book, then walks to Evensong in what might be Winchester Cathedral, returning to puzzle over 'the legend page' on which sparkle

> The stars of heaven, and angels' wings,
> Martyrs in a fiery blaze,
> Azure saints and silver rays,
> Moses' breastplate, and the seven
> Candlesticks John saw in heaven,
> The winged Lion of Saint Mark,
> And the Covenantal Ark,
> With its many mysteries
> Cherubim and golden mice.

Mark appeals to writers, being such a good writer himself. Some think that he was the young man who ran away naked when the Temple police grabbed the sheet he was wearing during the arrest of Jesus – they believe that this incident is his 'signature' to his Gospel. The last chapter is all movement, all quick happenings, and joy hurrying to displace fright and loss. It is like April weather in England when a burst of marvellous warmth disperses the 'aguish' climate. Mark is the kind of author who makes one turn the page, who forces the reader to keep up, who cries, 'Stay awake!'

Holy Cats

————◆————

Regular worshippers at Little Horkesley will have observed that as well as having a devoted choir, we also have a devout cat. I say 'devout' although many believe that his regular-as-clockwork appearance when the bell tolls has something to do with there being Whiskas in the vestry, a soft carpet in the sanctuary and soft laps in all directions. But as I say, who can doubt the goodness of this beautiful and well-behaved cat, and who can say that his deportment in church is not a lesson to us all? Long ago in Ireland a bishop's wife wrote a hymn for children, 'also suitable for adults', in which she mentioned 'All things wise and wonderful', and it is my opinion that this cat has entered himself, quite properly, in this category and thus joined our congregation. I would therefore like to quote in his honour some lines from the best cat-testimony ever written. They are the work of Christopher Smart, a friend of Dr Johnson, who also respected a cat.

My Cat, Jeoffry

For I will consider my Cat Jeoffry.

For he is the servant of the Living God, duly and daily
serving him.

For at the first glance of the glory of God in the East he
worships in his way.

For is this done by wreathing his body seven times round with
elegant quickness.

For then he leaps up to catch the musk, which is the blessing of
God upon his prayer.

For he rolls upon prank to work it in.

For having done duty and received blessing he begins to
consider himself.

For this he performs in ten degrees.

For first he looks upon his fore-paws to see if they are clean.

For secondly he kicks up behind to clear away there.

For thirdly he works it upon stretch with the fore-paws
extended.

For fourthly he sharpens his paws by wood.

For fifthly he washes himself. . . .

For tenthly he goes in quest of food.

For having consider'd God and himself he will consider
his neighbour.

For if he meets another cat he will kiss her in kindness. . . .

For when his day's work is done his business more
properly begins.

For he keeps the Lord's watch in the night against the
adversary.

How he counteracts the powers of darkness by his electrical
skin and glaring eyes.

For he counteracts the Devil, who is death, by brisking about
　　the life.
For in his morning orisons he loves the sun and the sun
　　loves him.
. . . For he purrs in thankfulness, when God tells him he's a
　　good Cat. . . .
For every house is incomplete without him . . .
For he knows that God is his Saviour.
For there is nothing sweeter than his peace when at rest.

As Don our cross-bearer will affirm, sometimes our worshipping cat has gone to sleep in his arms, and has not been
able to join in the Offertory hymn.

Just across the river from Little Horkesley, on the damp
north wall of Wiston Church, there is a thirteenth-century
painting of St Francis preaching to the birds. The birds sit
attentively in a tree, all facing west. This fresco was made
only twenty years or so after the saint's death at Assisi and
as a boy I would ponder his text. Perhaps, 'Are not five
sparrows sold for two farthings?' The Lord makes no mention of cats. But Jeremiah the sad young prophet does. A
devout cat knows its own history and our friend will know
that he follows a great tradition of church-going. He could
tell us, 'You have heard of church mice, so it follows that
you should have heard of church cats. We were a normal
sight hunting through the aisles at night and basking by the
graves by day, and joining in Tallis's Canon. That nursery
rhyme

> Hickory, dickory dock
> The mouse ran up the clock

is about a cat who lived in Exeter Cathedral, no less, in the seventeenth century, and who had a cat-flap carved for him in the door of the north transept by Bishop Cotton, so that he could un-mouse the clock chamber. Also in this cathedral you must have seen a very fine portrait of Tom, the verger's cat – a stone model, one-eyed and all, due to Tom's heroic fight with a rat.

My favourite holy cat belonged to Mother Julian at Norwich. She or he sits beside her in a stained-glass window. Anchoresses were permitted a window on the altar, a window on the world, a servant and a cat. Just the bare necessities. Mother Julian wrote a book called *The Revelations of Divine Love* which became a bestseller six hundred years later. I see her sharpening her goose-quill and writing, 'My vision declared the will of God to be that we should greatly value all his works, the noble nature of all creation and the excellency of man's creation', and her cat making sure that it was included.

A favourite walk of mine is in Morwenstow on the wild Cornish cliffs, Robert Hawker's old parish. Parson Hawker's parishioners were wreckers by trade. They – men and women alike – would murder some poor shipwrecked mariner for the ring on his finger. As for their harvest festivals, well, even Thomas Hardy admitted that there was no polite language in which to describe them. Some Victorian clergymen went to 'darkest Africa'; Parson Hawker went to where there was real savagery – in Cornwall. He outraged his parishioners by burying drowned sailors in Morwenstow graveyard and obliging the entire village to be mourners, and then by taking the harvest festival out of the barns and putting it into the church. He was exceedingly fond of cats, and ten of them followed him each Sunday to Matins and Evensong.

A beautiful white cat made his home in St Mary Redcliffe Church, Bristol in 1912 and chose a different lap each sabbath. His master was Eli Richards the verger. This cat died full of liturgical honours on St Thomas's Day 1927 and was given burial in the churchyard. When the organist, in passing, saw this church cat's grave being dug, he went in and played 'We love the place, O God' and 'Pleasant are thy courts above'. As St Mary's happened to be being repaired at the time, a stonemason was ordered to make a headstone to 'The Church Cat 1912–1927', where it can be seen to this day.

Another white cat, this one named Merbecke, resided in Old Warden Parish Church, Bedfordshire, during the 1970s. The kind vicar had found her bedraggled and half-starved on a bitter winter's night in 1972 and at first gave her a home in the vicarage. But Merbecke moved across to the church to enjoy the nice frowty odour of hangings and robes, and the unspeakable pleasures of the belfry.

Perhaps cats' eyes light up when a Cowper hymn is

announced. William Cowper was one of the rare people who could understand and come close to the fear and vulnerability of both wild and domestic creatures. Here is some of his poem called 'The Retired Cat'.

> A poet's cat, sedate and grave
> As poet well could wish to have,
> Was much addicted to inquire
> For nooks to which she might retire,
> And where, secure as mouse in chink,
> She might repose, and sit and think.

Cowper's cat and his pet hare slept together for eight years, and by them his spaniel Beau. When we give thanks to God for all his mercies, cats are bound to come high on the list. We know it and they know it. There is little that a cat doesn't know. Our own church cat knows when to process out – and when to come in again fast for the Whiskas. Coleridge in his *Rime of the Ancient Mariner* sums it up,

> He prayeth best, who loveth best
> All things both great and small;
> For the dear God who loveth us,
> He made and loveth all.

The essayist Montaigne questions the human pride which separates mankind from all things great and small. 'When I play with my cat, who knows but that she regards me more as a plaything than I do her? We amuse ourselves with our respective monkey-tricks. If I have my moments of

beginning and refusing, so she has hers.' St Francis insists
that they are our brothers and sisters. I must close with the
immortal Hodge. This is James Boswell speaking of Dr
Johnson's cat:

> I shall never forget the indulgence with which he
> treated Hodge, his cat; for whom he himself used to go
> out and buy oysters, lest the servants, having that trou-
> ble, should take a dislike to the poor creature. I am,
> unluckily, one of those who have an antipathy to a cat,
> so that I am uneasy when in the room with one, and I
> own that I frequently suffered a good deal from the
> presence of this same Hodge. I recollect him one day
> scrambling up Dr Johnson's breast, apparently with
> much satisfaction, while my friend, smiling and half-
> whistling, rubbed down his back, and pulled him by the
> tail, and when I observed he was a fine cat, saying,
> 'Why, yes, Sir, but I have had cats whom I liked better
> than this'; and then, as if perceiving Hodge to be out of
> countenance, adding, 'but he is a very fine cat, a very
> fine cat indeed.'

Immortality

— ◆ —

W hen we are alone we dwell continually on some things
and never on others, if we can help it. It is not
because certain subjects are too painful or awkward to con-
template, but because we no longer quite know what to
make of them. They have become a discarded part of our
religious language which no longer says to us what it
presumably said to our forefathers, so we leave it in a kind
of honoured abeyance. During its long and controversial
history the faith has gone through periods when all the talk
was of heaven, or of hell, or of love, or of guilt, or of doubt,
or of total belief. Or when all the talk was of – immortality!
'Immortal love', we sing, and 'Immortal, invisible'. Hymnwriters leave little in abeyance, and we sing things which we
dare not say.

Long ago, some of you will recall, there used to be glass
domes on the graves which were filled with snowy porcelain
flowers. They were called immortelles. Wrongly, of course,
for they eventually corroded and fell to pieces under the
wind and the rain, although they did last longer than cut
flowers. Among the porcelain flowers there would be porcelain hands clasping each other in an everlasting grip, and

porcelain texts about eternity. Although fragile, these sad, pretty churchyard ornaments did occasionally outlive the inscription on the tombstone, which again was no time at all.

At the sepulchre the angels said, 'He is not here, he is risen!' During the curious unreality of a friend's funeral I comforted myself with that 'He is not here.' Which immediately brought the question, 'Where is he then?' Well, we all know the answer to that – 'In heaven, of course.' I should have asked, '*What* is he now?' And then dared to have replied, 'Immortal.' Scripture never dodges this, one of the biggest of all questions. It is most explicit where this subject is concerned. 'Our citizenship is in heaven,' says St Paul, the man who once boasted that he was a citizen of no mean city, then meaning Rome. But we too have a dual nationality, this natural earth and that mysterious country of the redeemed. Our mistake has always been to have believed that our immortal life begins when our mortal life ends, when in fact these dual states of our being, the temporal and the eternal, run side by side from our birth.

The thought of death, that is the annihilation of time, is the most painful of all our painful thoughts, and it makes us frightened and miserable. We think of death as endless years, when it is a state where there can be no years, no centuries, no time at all. The Lord himself is timeless. Once, like us, he lived within time. He was born, he grew up, he accomplished his work, he was killed, and all within a young

Full Moon

man's lifetime. And then he entered timelessness and called it 'My Father's house'. It is the abode of truth and love. When his critics demanded further particulars of the future life, asking him what would happen to those who had married more than once, for example, he replied that with the resurrected there is no marriage and we 'are as the angels of God in heaven'. He was telling them that our earthly arrangements have no place there.

Our concept of the eternal has been greatly confused by poetic imagery, and by our finding it impossible to imagine ourselves where time does not exist. I am writing this on May Day, a time of spontaneous delight at being alive on earth, and beloved of mortals for as long as anyone can remember. A day which brought joy to the world for countless generations. And this brings me to that much-used religious word 'joy'. Joy, says the dictionary, is the climax of happiness. In both the New and Old Testaments it is a quality grounded on, and derived from, God himself. It should be the mark of the Christian and of Christian society. Peter once wrote of joy 'unspeakable', by which he meant a happiness so great that words failed him when it came to describing it. We each have our moments of unspeakable joy. They seem to come to us from nowhere, and it is often then that we catch a glimpse of the eternal. Saints and poets – and some are both – have striven to put this intense happiness into words, knowing that even at their most inspired these words fall short of what they actually saw and felt at some blissful moment. And each one of us, young and old, know what it is like momentarily to catch sight of something which has nothing to do with our mortality, something deathless, something 'divine'. And for a kind of measureless second, if there can be such a thing, we know that we have entered the realm of the *giver* of all that we call 'nature'.

Spiritual teachers such as St Paul frequently go out of their way to comfort those who despair at the limits of their vision. Do not worry: 'Now you see as in a glass, darkly, but then – face to face!' Paul's own first sight of Christ's kingdom was so dazzling that it blinded him. One minute he was a mere important official on the duty road, the next he was walking the road which Isaiah called the way of righteousness. From then on Paul would walk through the Roman empire *and* along the Lord's everlasting highway, at one and the same time. He would be in parallel sovereignties.

Jesus never said, 'You will enter my sovereignty when you die, that is if you are fit for it.' He told everyone he met, 'My kingdom is within you.' He too spoke of ineffable joy, that which the medieval hymnwriter calls 'those social joys beyond compare'. I have always been attracted by the contrasting moods of human life being likened to plants. In the Old Testament we have the elegiac image of men being cut down like grass and fading like flowers. In the New Testament we have the botanical accuracy of the Lord's contrasting human life with seeds which have to die in order to come up out of the ground, blossom and fruit. Time and time again he sees humanity as a wheatfield in an everlasting cycle of death and life.

For me, the most sublime description of the earthly paradise pre-figuring the paradise to come was written by a young clergyman who lived on the Welsh border in the seventeenth century, Thomas Traherne. It is in the book he wrote for a single reader, his friend Mrs Hopton, a married lady who he believed was tottering perilously between the Church of England and the Church of Rome. This book, now called *Centuries*, was made up of a series of instructional letters, the manuscript of which was found on a second-hand bookstall in London just before the First World War, and was first thought to be an undiscovered masterpiece by the poet Henry Vaughan. It created a literary sensation when it was published. Never before had the subject of joy received such joyous treatment. Here is Traherne's most famous description of joy. He remembers being a child in Hereford, a little city which had in fact suffered during the Civil War. But:

> All appeared new and strange at first, inexpressibly rare, and delightful and beautiful. I was a little stranger which at my entrance into the world was saluted and surrounded by innumerable joys. . . . My very ignorance was an advantage. . . . All things were joyful and precious. . . . All time was eternity, and a perpetual Sabbath. . . . The corn was orient and immortal wheat,

which should never be reaped, nor was ever sown. I thought it stood from everlasting to everlasting. The dust and stones of the street were as precious as gold. The gates were at first the end of the world, the green trees when I saw them first through one of the gates transported and ravished me; their sweetness and unusual beauty made my heart to leap. . . . The men! O what venerable and reverend creatures did the aged seem! Immortal cherubims! And young men glittering and sparkling angels, and maids strange seraphic pieces of life and beauty! Boys and girls tumbling in the streets, and playing, were moving jewels. I knew not that they were born and would die. But all things abided eternally as they were in their proper places. Eternity was manifest in the light of the day, and something infinite behind everything appeared. The city seemed to stand in Eden, or to be built in Heaven. The streets were mine, the Temple – Hereford Cathedral – was mine, the people were mine, the skies were mine . . . all the world was mine. . . . [But soon] I was corrupted and made to learn the dirty devices of this world. Which now I unlearn, and become as it were a little child again, that I may enter into the Kingdom of God.

Christ said, 'You will certainly have sorrow, but your sorrow will be turned to joy. I will see you again, and then you will have a joy which can never be taken from you.'

The Women
in the Lord's Life

It always comes as a slight shock to discover that one has been within touching distance of a person who has redirected history. The plant pathologist Stephen Garrett was among my earliest friends. I can see him now, eyes to the ground, half-listening to us whilst wholly engaged in searching for flowers. The Garrett family lived on the Suffolk coast where it had invented wonderful farm machinery and built Snape Maltings. It had also produced Stephen's 'cousin Lizzie' and 'cousin Millie', two sisters who helped to lay the foundations of today's women's movement. Cousin Lizzie was Elizabeth Garrett Anderson, Britain's first woman doctor – and woman mayor – and cousin Millie was Millicent Fawcett who helped to found women's colleges at Cambridge, and who was president of the great movement which eventually gave women the vote. Cousin Millie, as my old friend called her, was more familiar to me as the co-founder of the big tuberculosis hospital at Wiston, whose lights on the opposite bank of the Stour I can see from my garden. Those sad wards have now been turned into houses. When cousin Millie and her friend Dr Jane Walker built their hospital TB was the AIDS of its day. As children we would bike past it, staring in bewilderment at the rows of long prams set out in the snow, and in the prams – grown-ups! I remember their thin hands waving to us.

Both of the Garrett sisters had a hard time. It was then thought scandalous for women to be doctors and foolish for them to vote. As for them having a university education, this was thought very dangerous. It is a famous tale of struggle, and here was I, a young man in his twenties, talking to someone whose cousins were in the thick of it.

I mention these distant and yet close liberated women because of the saint whose feast day we celebrate at this time of year, Mary Magdalen. She is the epitome of Christ's liberating attitude towards the women of his day. Unlike the Garrett sisters and their sisters in the movement, Mary of Magdala was not a respectable woman and people were shocked by Jesus's friendship with her. She got her name from Magdala, a fishing village on the shore of Galilee, and its location might be said to have made her the woman she was because it lay halfway between the sophisticated new town of Tiberias and the Roman garrison at Capernaum. Christian tradition places her among the immoral and those who are beyond the pale. The Gospels talk of her being possessed by devils, by which they mean that she was driven by instincts which were out of her control. Jesus had made Capernaum his headquarters after he had been driven from home and it may have been then that Mary from nearby Magdala had first encountered him. She, along with other women, 'followed him'. That is, she followed his teachings, his law, and these transformed her life. The Jesus who liberated women from 'devils' is the wise leader who set them free from all kinds of man-made restrictions, from mental illness, from customs which imprisoned them. It is a Jesus whom the Church has played down, which prefers its women to be 'pure and holy' to them being what they are, female, and all that this state naturally and spiritually – and intellectually – implies. Yet when we read about the ladies mentioned in the New Testament, and there are many of them and most of them named, they appear as anything other than the images of them that we see in paintings and poetry.

Before we remind ourselves of the real Mary of Magdala, as she appears in the Gospels, let us first take a glance at Christ's revolutionary attitude towards women generally. The first instance of this comes in St Matthew's account of a Canaanite who rushes at him, making a noise and, as everyone else thought, making herself a nuisance. A typically hysterical woman, his disciples believed. They were quick to advise him to have nothing to do with her. 'Send her away – see how she comes shouting after us!' And at first Jesus himself seems to step back from her demands, telling her that his duty is toward the lost sheep of *Israel* 'and to them alone'. But the Canaanite woman is not going to have any of this tribal evasiveness. Her daughter is being tormented by a devil – disease? Something in her character urging her to lead a bad life? We are not told. But whatever it is, it has made her mother desperate. She doesn't care what people think of her behaviour. She pushes her way to Christ and says, 'Help me, Sir.' And he helps her.

Nearly all Jesus's radical answers to women's questions are brought about by chance encounters. His ministry is peripatetic and thus he runs into women who are either going about their domestic tasks or who, having heard about his cures, waylay him. He is a saviour who is always on the move. And Palestine is a little country and his fame goes before. The easy access to him which women have is itself a cause of gossip and criticism. He challenges myths and superstitions, and thus challenges the whole social structure of the male–female order. One woman tells him, 'No man ever spoke to me like this before.' Then a woman with menstrual difficulties, and who is thus 'unclean', dares to touch him, herself the untouchable. It is no more than the brush of her hand against the hem of his robe as he is jostled along by the vociferous Eastern crowd, but he feels it. Feels his power leaving him in order to empower her as it enters her plight. Her haemorrhage suddenly stops – she can feel it, the cleanness returning. She will be able to take her place in society once more. He has dealt with the loneliness that illness had thrust upon her.

Then we have capable ladies like Joanna and Susanna who

see that thirteen weary walkers have a good meal and beds for the night, and who provide for them, as St Luke says, 'out of their own resources'. Joanna was the wife of King Herod's steward, and presumably well-off and influential. And of course there are Mary and Martha who provided a kind of safe house for Jesus, a place where he could escape from those who followed him about and exhausted him. Although even there, in this blessed spot, domesticity could get in the way of more important matters. Poor Martha, how one's heart goes out to her! A window in one of our churches shows her without a halo, and her sister with one. I do not think that the Lord meant that. It is what I would call glazier's theology.

Jesus's most fascinating encounter with a woman was when he was walking in Samaria. He was resting by Jacob's well early in the morning when this woman arrives with her water-pot and he asks her to give him a drink. She is astonished. Jews and Samaritans were not allowed to drink from the same cup. He says that if she only knew who he really was, it would be her asking him for refreshment, and he says those unforgettable words: 'Whosoever drinketh of this water shall thirst again. But whosoever drinketh of the water that I shall give him shall never thirst . . . the water that I shall give him shall be in him a well of water springing up into everlasting life.'

The woman is at this stage of their meeting rather like Martha in that her housewifely common sense takes precedence over religious talk, although being a Samaritan, she would have listened to the latter day in, day out. She asks this stranger to give her this water which quenches thirst for ever, for then she won't have to fetch and carry water from Jacob's well every day. The talk then grows personal but the woman is not offended. She is much married and used to men. Again, we have Jesus associating with a woman who one would not expect to see with a spiritual leader. This woman by the well is a bit like the Wife of Bath in *The Canterbury Tales*, jolly and far from respectable.

When the disciples return from shopping in Sychar, the town where the woman lives, they warn him against her. 'Why do you talk with *her?*'

Why? Because she will not keep the wonderful things he told her to herself but will act as a carrier of his message to her own people – 'Come, see a man, which told me all things that I ever did: is not this the Christ?' As for the disciples, they would have been taught a vital lesson. Jesus was not for Jews alone.

And so to that extraordinary woman Mary of Magdala – the Magdalen. The woman with a past and a future, for she was the first human being to see the resurrected Jesus, the Christ indeed. She, and all the saints, become clichés and calendar marks if we do not bring our intelligence to bear on their reality. If her past was as sensational as religious gossip implies, then it was also rather ordinary. It was what happened to her after her encounter with Jesus which overwhelms us. Such courage had she, such devotion, such love – such a total rehabilitation. She faced what many of the Lord's male friends were unable to face, his execution. She summoned up enough strength to assist at the burial of the shocking remains. Mary and two other women, Salome and James's mother, had all accompanied Jesus when he travelled to Jerusalem for his terrible death. Thus the Magdalen saw it all, saw it all through from the beginning to the end. She watched as Joseph of Arimathea lowered the body into a sheet which he had brought for this purpose and had it carried to his own tomb. Immediately the Sabbath was over, on Sunday morning when it was still dark, Mary, Salome and James's mother, another Mary, went to the grave to clean the body with oil and to lay it out. If the Magdalen was the same woman – some believe she was – who had anointed the Beloved's feet with spikenard, afterwards drying them with her hair, a surprisingly sensuous act to those present, then she would have remembered those dear feet before they were mutilated. The crux of that sensational tale is often missed. The Magdalen, once maybe an outcast, anoints Christ in the house of a leper, a well-to-do person but also an outcast, and those who associate with either of them are taking a risk.

Those women who threw in their lot with Elizabeth Garrett Anderson and her sister Millicent Fawcett lost their respectability and gained great things.

O Comforter, Draw Near

———◆———

Christ's inner circle had such a brief apprenticeship for what it had to do, just three years. Three years in which to train to change the world. During this training period it was full of fears, full of inadequacies, and often feeling both sure and yet unsure of its capabilities. Now and then there were episodes where people over-reached themselves, which was scary and humiliating. When we read the Acts of the Apostles or the history of the beginning of the Church, we are moved as much by the failings as by the triumphs of these men. They are so like us, and yet so unlike us, being the commissioned officers of Jesus. At first their dependency on him makes them vulnerable to fright verging on terror. While he was with them they could be childlike, even a little absurd. In what order would they sit at the top table in heaven? A mother spoke up for her sons. One should be on his right, the other on his left. They would imitate his healing method, only to find that it did not always work. Once the police were called in. Their Lord chided them, coached them, taught them and, as we do when we try to educate a child, would say, 'Wake up!' or 'How dull you are!'

Often his words went over their heads and then they would protest, 'But we do *not* know the way!' to be answered with, 'I am the way, the truth and the life. He who follows me will be on the path to the Kingdom.'

And then there was the dread question which none of them dare ask – 'What will happen to us when he leaves us? When we are on our own?'

This question did not vanish when he told them such wonderfully reassuring things as, 'And lo, I am with you always, even to the end of time.' For what did this mean? He was so mysterious. He spoke their simple language and yet another language too, one not heard before.

'Talk plainly,' they said. How could he go and yet stay? How could he remain with them on earth and yet be gone from them?

There was the worrying matter of their failings and unworthiness. What was all too evident was his greatness and their smallness. One of the worst proofs of it was when he and John and James and Peter, the 'advanced disciples', left the rest of them at the foot of Mount Hermon whilst they climbed to a high place to witness his Transfiguration, only to find a dangerous situation on their return. Those below had attempted to cure an epileptic boy and nothing had happened. They had done what they had so often seen Jesus do, and nothing had come of it. The crowd booed and they were about to be arrested as quacks. And then Jesus returned and the lad was healed immediately.

'Why couldn't we do it?' they asked, crestfallen and shocked.

'Because your faith is small. Why, if you only had a mustard-seed-sized faith you would have been able to move this mountain!' They would have looked up to the top of the very hill of his radiance.

All the time the Twelve had been his company they had fretted and worried themselves about his power not filling them as it should. How could they continue his teaching? Clearly, they were without his authority. And thus the nagging, faithless question of what would happen to them when he left. Then came Pentecost. Well, they did understand Pentecost – and Passover, and Tabernacles, all the great Jewish feasts of the fields. To celebrate that year's Pentecost the Eleven had run a lottery to make up their number to the perfect dozen, 'and the lot fell upon Matthias'. This done, reports Luke, the house in which they were gathered in all their holy completion was filled with a sound like a mighty rushing wind and their heads with fiery tongues which were able to convey the gospel to every hearer, no matter their nationality. 'Every man heard them speak of Christ in his own language.' And they were only Galileans.

Everybody was not impressed. Some said they were drunk. 'At this time of the morning?' said Peter.

Jerusalem was packed for Pentecost, as it was for all the harvest festivals. It was a multinational city full of people from all round the Mediterranean. It was to this diverse crowd that the disciples, who must now be called apostles, first preached the gospel. It marked among other things the end of Babel. In some extraordinary way what was said was understood, no matter that Parthians, Medes, Libyans, Arabs and Cretans were listening. And here Peter preached his great sermon. He stood up and raised his voice, says Luke. It was not a planned sermon but a spontaneous utterance of all that Christ had taught him during those long walks through the countryside. He quoted the rural prophet Joel:

> And it shall come to pass in the last days, saith God, I will pour out of my Spirit upon all flesh: and your sons and your daughters shall prophesy, and your young men shall see visions, and your old men shall dream dreams. And on my servants and on my handmaidens I will pour out in those days of my Spirit; and they shall prophesy.

(Acts 2.17–18, KJV)

It was with these words of Joel, reiterated by Peter, that the Church began. He saw it continuing 'to all who are far off', or ourselves all these many years later. At Pentecost in Jerusalem the infant Church suddenly realized that the Comforter so bafflingly spoken of by Christ was nothing less than the very breath of God, the essential spiritual element which would keep it alive.

Around our village churches the trees toss and susurrate, and the sun is warming the old stones. We shall soon be listening to Bach's Whitsun Cantatas. Whitsun wedding flowers scent the aisles. When Peter was preaching they would have been harvesting the first corn for the Pentecostal offering, but ours blows like grass still.

Peter-Paul
at Little Horkesley

———◆———

We know more about the character and personality of Peter than of any other apostle except Paul. This church is dedicated to the two men who were foremost in the foundation of Christianity, each of them complex and difficult. Neither at first seemed at all worthy or suitable for the great authority which would be given them. Indeed, had they gone through our interview procedures for a high position in a religious establishment they would have been turned down flat. They had what we would call 'personality problems'. Peter was impulsive and inclined to have to eat his words. Paul was scrupulous in the wrong way, a carrier-out of orders, and pitiless. He was zealous. Peter was a fisherman but not a 'simple' fisherman. Paul was a tent-maker whose letters betray a brilliant education and culture. Peter was indigenous, a very local man whose entire world was little Galilee. Paul was an experienced traveller who came from a busy city which had grown up on one of the trade routes of the ancient world. Peter belonged to Palestine. Paul was proud to belong to Rome itself. Peter was groomed, as we would say, for his immense role by Jesus himself. Paul came to Jesus by a sudden blinding conviction of who he really was.

Peter's weaknesses were the common weaknesses of us all, easily understood, easily forgiven. His denial of Christ in the quite terrifying circumstances in which it took place, though also terrible, is comprehensible. Had we witnessed the crosses planted around Roman towns for the execution of local trouble-makers, would we have been brave? When Peter cries so bitterly for letting down the person who meant everything to him, we weep too, knowing only too well the self-disgust which comes from cowardice.

Paul's weakness, on the other hand, is not a common weakness, not one which we are likely to possess. Paul was a persecutor, a hounder-out of the enemies of the system. He could stand guard over the clothes when Stephen's executioners stripped off to free their arms for his stoning. We know that after his conversion Paul suffered dreadfully because of what he had done – had been. He never sought to justify his past. 'I am what I am,' he said, meaning a man who had been redeemed. 'Once I was blind but now I can see!' To be merciless and cruel for any reason is to be blind.

'Who are you?' he was to ask the being who had blinded him physically as he dutifully journeyed into Damascus.

The answer was concise. 'I am Jesus whom you have been persecuting.'

We then learn that Paul's conscience has been pricking

him for some time and that he is not as hardened to his task as those who employed him would have liked him to be. Animals were goaded along by sharp nails set in wood and soon learned how useless it was to kick against the pricks.

The horror is that, had not Paul's eyes been opened, he would have been the agent sent back to Jerusalem to destroy Peter and the Church's first converts. Indeed, they would have been awaiting his return from Damascus with prayer and fear. Neither Peter nor Paul could have ever imagined their linked names, their joined destinies under the Lord – or that between them they would change the world. The infant Church must have taken nervous stock of the pair of them. Could this able preacher be clumsy, well-meaning, argumentative and all-too-human Peter? Can this be wicked Saul from Tarsus who would once have hanged his own grandfather, given the order? The rest of the apostles had only one question where Saul, now calling himself Paul, was concerned. It was, can we trust him? Regarding Peter, they remembered the Lord's play on his name, Petras – rock. There would have been an exchange of looks when Jesus declared, 'On this rock will I build my church!' Peter! That fairweather friend! Christ's knowledge of us, his being able to see what none of us can ever see, is the ultimate recognition of who and what we are. Not sharing this, there must have been more than one amongst the Twelve mulling over Peter's failings and Paul's crimes.

Who was Peter? Why did Jesus tell him, 'Follow me'?

Peter was a seeker, a spiritual man who had not then found what he needed. He sought for God as he worked the fishing boats, the God who had eluded him in the conventional religion to which he belonged. A wonderful teacher had walked along the shore and said two words, 'Follow me.' What Peter heard was, 'I will lead you to where you want to go.' It was, 'Drop everything, leave home, come with me.' It took Peter a long time to see God in Jesus. His gradual awakening – so unlike Paul's lightning flash of comprehension – is that of most of us. Which is why we find everything about Peter so moving, so applicable to ourselves. He was frequently scolded by Jesus for his slow grasp of what was before his very eyes. 'How dull you are!' And then, one upsetting day, 'You will not always have me with you!'

Peter is called the Prince of the Apostles but Paul, had he had his way, would not have called himself an apostle at all. Yet the Church has united these men in their greatness from the beginning. Thus we have the double dedication of our country church. Very popular they were long ago in this Essex–Suffolk realm. It is Peter-Paul at St Osyth, at Clare, at glorious Lavenham, at West Mersea, Eye, Aldeburgh – a whole gazetteer of their linked patronage lies all around us. One can hear the medieval parishioners saying, 'Let's have them both for safety's sake!'

'Apostle' means 'one sent'. Twelve men, most of them in the ordinary way stay-at-homes, were sent out into the wide world by Christ himself carrying with them nothing but his teachings. Peter's primacy among them lay in Christ's understanding of his strength and his slow, firm recognition of who he was. The Jews longed for one of their great prophets to return and bring them national freedom, and the disciples hazarded their names when Jesus asked them, 'Who do people say I am?'

'And you,' he asked Peter, 'who do *you* think I am?'

Everything – the whole veracity of the Church – depended on his giving the right answer. If this most clear-sighted of all his friends still had not grasped the identity of the person they had followed all this time, then who could?

'And you, who do you think I am?'

'You,' answered the blunt fisherman, 'you are the anointed one, the Son of the living God!'

Jesus was overwhelmed. Truth, shared recognition, joy, relief, flooded through the little group. And it was during this famous moment of Christian vision that Jesus made a pun on Peter's name and told him, 'You are Peter the rock, and on this rock I will build my church, and death will never conquer it!'

In spite of suffering every kind of destructive force, including the worst of all, indifference, the Church lives. It lives because of country parishes such as ours, mere pebbles in comparison to Peter's rock, being part of its life. During the last lesson which Jesus taught his chief disciple, he changes the metaphor. He makes Peter a shepherd. Fishermen and shepherds are poles apart and Peter must have felt rather bewildered. Having saved souls from the depths, Peter would have to nourish them. He and the Lord have just finished having breakfast on the beach when the questioning starts.

'Simon son of John, do you love me above all else?'
'Yes, Lord, you know that I love you.'
'Then feed my lambs.'

'Simon son of John, do you love me?'
'Yes, Lord, you know I love you.'
'Then tend my sheep.'

'Simon son of John, do you love me?'
'Lord, you *know* I love you – you know everything.'
'Feed my sheep.'

Little Horkesley's name – and Great Horkesley's too – comes from the Old English word 'hurk'. A hurk was a temporary shelter for lambs. To keep the lambs in the ordinary hurdles were woven with straw.

'Simon son of John, do love me above all else?'
'Yes, Lord, you know that I love you.'
'Then feed my lambs.'

The Strong Name of the Trinity

A nd so we come to Trinity Sunday. On Trinity Sunday we are not expected to work out the complexity of God, Father, Son and Holy Spirit, but to acknowledge as best we can the wholeness of the Creator. We ourselves, after all, consist of many elements. How often we hear of someone who is seen in only physical terms, usually someone who is beautiful. The media present a daily parade of such individuals. Their bodies are set before us but rarely their minds. And there are those whose intelligence is always mentioned, but never their persons. Yet they have bodies. And then there are those who exist in our imagination *sans* flesh or brains, who are neither beautiful nor clever, only good. Thus humanity itself is popularly viewed as a 'trinitarian' construct.

An ancient hymn calls the Trinity 'the unity of three-fold light', and we need go no further in God-description. The most celebrated Trinity hymn is Reginald Heber's 'Holy, Holy, Holy, Lord God Almighty'. Heber is quoting from the revelation of heaven which St John had whilst working in a salt-mine out of which he saw a vision of eternal adoration of the Author of all things. It is from this vision that all our concepts of God and his dwelling-place descend. Reginald Heber's hymn makes us join in the mighty acknowledgement made by heaven itself of the triune One. Heber was a poet-parson from the north who knew Sir Walter Scott and who felt himself pulled this way and that by his duty as a priest and his love of literature, with the result that he often over-worked, especially when they made him Bishop of Calcutta in 1822. His diocese was nothing less than the whole of British India. In four years it killed him. Not only did Reginald Heber preach and confirm throughout this vast area but he left behind at his death at the age of forty-three much travel-writing and verse. He was one of the first hymnwriters to compose a set of hymns for the Church's seasons. We less-striving Christians of the twenty-first century look back on Bishop Heber and his like with a kind of wonder at what made them not only tick, but race!

On Trinity Sunday we recognize that we are in the three-fold hands of one who is Redeemer, Comforter and King. St John's vision of him is total in its magnificence and tenderness. 'And I John saw the holy city, new Jerusalem, coming down from God out of heaven, prepared as a bride adorned for her husband (India would have confirmed this image for Heber). And I heard a great voice out of heaven saying,

> 'Behold, the tabernacle of God is with men, and he will dwell with them, and they shall be his people, and God himself shall be with them, and be their God. And God shall wipe away all tears from their eyes; and there shall

be no more death, neither sorrow, nor crying, neither
shall there be any more pain: for the former things are
passed away.'

(Revelation 21.2, 3–4, KJV)

Trinity Sunday is a comparatively recent feast in the long
history of the Church. The Holy Trinity was not officially
honoured until the Middle Ages, and that was chiefly
brought about because Thomas Becket, then England's most
popular saint, was consecrated a bishop on that day. Christ
himself put its meaning in a nutshell. Talking in private to
Councillor Nicodemus, that furtive seeker after truth, he
said, 'God so loved the world that he gave his only son, to
the end that all who believe in him should not die but live
eternally.' To this he added, whilst speaking to less cautious
friends, 'I will pray to my Father, and he will give you
another Comforter, that he may abide with you for ever. . . .
So let not your hearts be troubled. Peace, I leave with you,
my peace I give you.' The Lord's words set no conundrum.
The three-foldness of God is shown unmysteriously.

Not that Nicodemus found it at all simple. He was a
literalist and religious conservative who until he sought out
Jesus had obeyed the laws and customs of his faith to the
letter. It is a great comfort to live with a firm religious structure. But it made Nicodemus curious about what existed
outside it. If someone outside his 'church' could do good
things, then he 'must have God with him'.

However, he waited till it was dark before coming to the

house of the Lord. We then have an example of his inflexible mind. For when he is told that he must be born again, he replies, 'How absurd! How can a man re-enter the womb?' And Jesus's metaphor, so easily understood by the masses, though not always by those closest to him, was a hindrance to the legalistic Nicodemus, member of the Grand Council.

But Jesus refuses to change the way in which he teaches all of us, bright or not so bright. 'You ought not to be astonished when I speak as I do. The wind blows where it wills. You hear the sound of it, but you don't know where it comes from or where it goes. So it is with everyone who is born of the Spirit.' And we hear once again that house-shaking Pentecostal gale of the Holy Spirit, the very life-breath of Christ blowing through the world, through Time, through eternity.

There would soon come a time when Nicodemus, filled with God's own breath, or the spirit of Christ, all his caution fled, would no longer wait for night to fall before hastening to his Saviour. He became quite reckless – he, a pillar of the Government, taking instruction from an itinerant teacher with heretical views on the old religion. The teacher who made him and great numbers of other people members of a kingdom which lay beyond all earthly control.

Two figures emerge from the readings for Holy Trinity, one secretive, the other open and challenging, one didactic, the other wildly poetic, one set in his ways, the other shout-ing, 'Make way! Make way for someone whose sandals I am not worthy to do up!' The conventional man and the young man who said that all he was – was a voice! A herald. Councillor Nicodemus and John the Baptist. Two men who would never have been able to say an intelligible word to each other once upon a time.

The last reference to Nicodemus is poignant. He and another distinguished person who had much to fear from 'association with a blasphemer', as we might put it, had come together to give an executed friend a decent funeral, else the bloody remains would have been left for the birds. Joseph provided a grave safe from scavengers – his own, as it happened – Nicodemus 'about a hundred pounds of myrrh and aloes'. 'Then took they the body of Jesus, and wound it in linen cloths with spices, as the manner of the Jews is to bury.' It was not just the Second Person of the Trinity which lay in the cold tomb all night, but all three aspects of God, its 'Unity unshaken', as another old hymn puts it.

Walking

———◆———

I have been wondering what the Suffolk farmers of my boyhood would have made of our modern church custom of the 'farm walk'. What would they have said had they been told that the whole congregation was going to tour their fields and yards on a Sunday afternoon in early summer? Rogation, yes, they all knew about Rogation, but a walk round a farm? It was they who did the farm-walking on a Sunday afternoon, not the vicar and his lot. They did it winter and summer, freezing or sweating. Dressed in their Sunday-best and often accompanied by their wives, and always by their dogs, they took stock – and not only of their own crops but of their neighbour's too. The most popular image of a farmer was of him leaning on a gate to stare across his acres. Their farm walks took place between Sunday dinner and Sunday tea, both vast meals, and the latter very sociable. At this time of the year, post harvest, they would encounter blackberrying and nuttings, sloe-ing and wild fruiting generally. Our most blissful find would be bullaces, those hedge plums which made nice sharp jam. On the farm itself there was only necessary work such as milking and feeding. The atmosphere was sedate and noticeably quiet. Quietest of all were the courting couples lying well off the main route of the Sunday walkers, for the one thing which young people could not do in the parents' homes was 'court'. Discreet as foxes, they rustled like aspens and were passed in silence.

The other walking was to morning and evening service and to Sunday School. The mileage was impressive. Sunday kept you as much on your feet as on your knees and was never the day of rest. But it was an obviously special day; the very air told us so. It smelled different, looked different, and we were different during it. Samuel Palmer has caught the walking from the service to perfection, the stateliness of the group with the sermon still buzzing in its collective head, the best clothes, the freedom from labour. Like Millet's fieldworkers hearing the Angelus, they show their souls. They are rapt.

There used to be a simple old hymn which went:

> When we walk with the Lord,
> In the light of his word,
> What a glory he sheds on our way!

Remembering those words makes me think of the famous analogy of physical and spiritual progress.

'I am the way,' said Jesus.

'And a highway shall be there, and a way. And it shall be called the way of holiness, it shall be for wayfaring men, and the redeemed shall walk there,' said Isaiah.

Walking

The Old Testament begins with a man walking with God and the New Testament has Christ's life here ending with a walk along the Emmaus road. The divine companionship of Eden was renewed in the Jerusalem countryside. We are taught to think about the disgraced Eden-dwellers but not about the loneliness of God when there was no more companionship for him in the garden in the cool of the evening. The risen Christ did not appear to his friends as an awesome being but as a simple walker. Mary Magdalen encountered him 'walking in the garden'. The unnamed disciples he caught up on the Emmus road, like her, could not imagine him walking.

This tramping-along Christ offers a perfect concept of life's hard, cheerful, relentless road. 'O for a closer walk with God!' cried poor William Cowper when mental illness seemed to drag him behind. Two or three times he fancied himself so far in the rear, so distant from his Friend, that he thought of killing himself. Illness causes us to lose step, to lose contact. Walking is famously curative. I once gave a talk to a room full of country clergymen in Norfolk and recommended that they should walk their parishes because (a) it was quite the best way to stay happy and healthy, and (b) it was an easy, natural way to know and be known. They laughed. I told them the old Latin tag *solvitur ambulando* – you can work it out by walking – and they thought they might give it a try. Cars and incumbents should not always go by together in a kind of blinding flash.

The companionable path – what could be better? The scenery passes very slowly so that we not only see it but smell it, and feel it under our feet. Knotty problems unravel with the miles. Mind and body, imagination and plain fact, step it out harmoniously. Should I feel writer's block coming on, I do not sit ripping failed sheets out of the type-writer, as authors do on television: I go out and walk. I tell myself, '*Solvitur ambulando!*' The historian G. M. Trevelyan used to say, 'I have two doctors, my left leg and my right.' And some of the poets, Coleridge, Wordsworth and their circle, did all their best work on the hoof, the act of walking and the act of composition becoming synonymous.

Often, the most fruitful walk is the alone walk. Yet at the same time, neither alone nor lonely. For we commune with everything we pass, everything we see. And there is often the Other – the ever-companionable Christ. The friendship is a rather daring assumption but we have to remember that he became Man in order to be intimate with his creation. His healing powers and storytelling apart, what happiness it must have been for those men and women, boys and girls – always lots of children – to walk the familiar paths with the Lord. William Blake was so overwhelmed by this thought that he wrote:

> And did those feet in ancient time
>   Walk upon England's mountains green?
> And was the holy Lamb of God
>   On England's pleasant pastures seen?

This companionable Jesus trod the West End streets with Blake, the pure white Lamb of God among the sooty buildings. Blake wanted the 'doors of perception cleaned' so that his fellow Londoners could also walk with their Lord along the Strand or out of the smoke and through Islington. The walking Christ was both his London friend and his New Jerusalem friend – this is how Blake saw him.

The Incarnation is the restoration of the ancient friendship between God and man. 'I am with you always, even to the ends of the earth.' As Christians we walk in the way of the Lord, as best we can. In the Old Testament only the greatest, holiest of men, the prophets, had God's ear and 'walked' *with* him. Everyone else had to be content with walking in his ways and according to his ordinances. But when Jesus was born in Bethlehem everything changed. The worst of companions could tread alongside him. It caused scandal. 'Don't you know the kind of people you are walking with?' they said. 'Crooks, prostitutes . . . *Samaritans*?' All the same, they saw him make the lame to walk, the spiritually crippled to step it out with a new confidence. There is no isolated walker on his path. The milestones of the years pass but with Christ we move along in the timelessness of his friendship, saying to ourselves, 'So shall my walk be close with God' and finding it to be the most natural thing on earth.

A Weathered Man

Not only is scripture set in time and place, but also in weather. Its characters are rained on, blown about in gales, baked in deserts, chilled, made happy by fine days. It is another way of their being like us. We like to imagine that we are the result of our native climate, be it the Congo or the Mediterranean, the Arctic or the West Country. Too much rain and too little sun, or the reverse, makes its mark on us just as it does on a building or a field.

'I hear, Sir, that in your country you worship the sun,' said a Scottish lady to the Shah of Persia during his visit to Edinburgh long ago.

'And so would you, Madam, if you ever saw it,' he replied.

We in eastern England live in what is called a marine climate, in counties kept fresh by winds blowing in from the North Sea. It polishes our faces and nips around our bones and keeps us 'on the go'. As we pass we tell each other what the weather is – 'Cold today' – or if it happens to be at all excessive, we ask, 'How do you like this?' On the whole our weather is equable though ever changing. As John Constable, the best weather painter, told us, 'No two days are the same', allowing us to point out these changes as we

Saint Swithun's Day

pass one another in the village, just in case by an off-chance they might be missed. Certainly they are the most missed things when we leave this country for a costa. Phenomenal weather is rare, the 1976 summer, the 1987 gale, the terrible snows of 1947. Historians know about Dickensian winters and the endless rains of the 1880s which wrecked British agriculture – washed it away. But on the whole if our Saxon ancestors could put in a reappearance they would sniff our air and say, 'East Anglia!'

As I muse about all this on a July day, the West-Saxon weatherman who comes to mind is St Swithun:

> St Swithun's day, if thou dost rain,
> For forty days it will remain;
> St Swithun's day, if thou be fair,
> For forty days it will be fair.

The saint would not have been pleased to be commemorated in this jingle either for its style or its statement. He would not have liked to be the leader of those obscure saints which superstition has turned into seaweed-like weather forecasters. It would have annoyed him to have the realities of his life obscured by a myth – though such is the fate of many good people, to go down in history as either the victim of a single indiscreet action or of a popular legend – because this should be not to be known at all. Yet through the centuries the Church positively encouraged a limited view of its saints. It was enough simply to recognize them by some attribute, some tale. The remarkable man or woman behind this shorthand sign had a life which soon became indecipherable, all its fullness lost in the fog of Time. The lives of the saints can be brief lives indeed.

St Swithun's life ended on 2 July 862 – no one knows when it began. He was the Bishop of Winchester and a builder not only of churches but of bridges, roads and gates. He was a walker who, whenever he had to consecrate a new church, would make his way to it on foot, and often at night, in imitation of that Walker on the road to Emmaus, unrecognized by those he met on the way but showing all the same humble signs of his being no ordinary traveller. His last wish was to be buried in the pathway to his cathedral so that he would be close to his friends as they walked to the services, their footsteps on his grave. And where, in his own words, the raindrops from the cathedral eaves would fall on him. There he lay for over a century, as he had commanded, until another bishop had him exhumed, taken inside and placed in a magnificent shrine which attracted such hordes of pilgrims that the monks got rather fed up with him, his cult making so much work. In St Swithun's day his minster was called St Peter's House but now they called it after him. (At the Reformation they renamed it after the Holy Trinity.) It was on 15 July 971 that they dug up the rain saint. And so what we have here is a practical and unpretentious bishop who liked the notion of becoming a fragment of the path which led into his church, lying under the north wall, the water shooting from its thatch as it had splashed around him during his solitary walks through Wessex.

Among the realities of the gospel are those accounts of Christ existing in the natural climatic conditions of Palestine, the hot days, the bitter nights. In Shakespeare's *Cymbeline* a brother mourns a brother with words which would not have been inappropriate at Calvary.

> Fear no more the heat o' the sun,
> Nor the furious winter's rages,
> Thou thy worldly task hast done,
> Home art gone and ta'en thy wages.

In all reverence it could have been said by one of the Lord's 'brothers' at the foot of the Cross. The hardships of his three years on the road, weatherwise, have not always been properly understood. After the debacle at the Nazareth synagogue he never knew again the actual shelter which a house provides. Like Swithun and so many of his followers, he was on the road in all weathers. There is a collect in which we ask God 'that we may so pass through things temporal, that we finally lose not the things eternal', and it reminds us of Jesus in the desert. When a little later on religious men asked him to prove himself by showing them a sign from heaven, he used a weather analogy – one used by us to this day. 'When it is evening, you say it will be fair weather, for the sky is red. And in the morning, it will be foul weather today, for the sky is red and lowering. O you hypocrites! You can discern the face of the sky, but you cannot discern the signs of the times.' St Swithun would have liked the way he ended the Sermon on the Mount: 'Love your enemies, so that you can become the children of God – the God who makes the sun to rise on the evil and the good, and who sends rain upon the just and the unjust.' Here both sun and rain are recognized as universal blessings. Of course we often have to put up with more of one kind than the other. To quote Shakespeare again:

> A great while ago the world begun,
> With hey, ho, the wind and the rain;
> For the rain it raineth every day.

On the Feast
of the Transfiguration
at Mount Bures

⸺◄►⸺

Our man-made mount rises just a few yards away from the church of St John the Baptist, Mount Bures. On it the blackberry blossom fades and the reeling oak trees cling to its sandy soil for dear life. Almost as familiar to us are the mountains of Christ in Palestine, Carmel, Gilboa, Hermon, Sinai, Tabor, places which raise our sights. Mount Hermon was chosen by Jesus to allow the three of the friends who were closest to him to see him as his Father saw him. Only the great Christian poets are able to give some kind of explanation of what occurred. Here is St John of the Cross:

> The farther that I climbed the height
> The less I seemed to understand
> The cloud so tenebrous and grand
> That there illuminates the night.
> For he who understands that sight
> Remains for aye, though knowing naught,
> Transcending knowledge with his thought.

> . . . This summit all so steeply towers
> And is of excellence so high
> No human faculties or powers
> Can ever to the top come nigh.

The poet is not specifically writing about the Trans-figuration as Christians try to understand it, but about how faith can take us to realities for which there are no explan-ations. They happen – but what happened? Transfiguration is a fascinating word, but what does it mean? The Gospels tell of a moment on Mount Hermon when Jesus was 'trans-figured'. They say that 'his face shone like the sun', and, more down to earth, that his clothes became dazzling white with a whiteness no bleacher could equal. Luke notes: 'While he was praying the appearance of his face changed.' Does 'transfiguration' mean that Jesus suffered metamor-phosis, being turned into something which was no longer human? The Greek and Roman gods had a long history of such changes. But the whole point of the Transfiguration is that Jesus remained a man. What he did was to make his divinity visible to his fellow men, Peter, James and John. William Blake imagined the scene when, in 'Jerusalem', he asks,

> And did the countenance divine
> Shine forth upon our clouded hills?

Every now and then some verse in a hymn jumps out at us. At the Transfiguration I often remember the plea,

Anoint and cheer our soilèd face
With the abundance of thy grace.

Perhaps the disciples compared their appearance with that of Christ. The hymn reminds us that life can be a grubby business. That we know, that we feel. And in a way we accept it – that life makes us grey. What shabby creatures we are in comparison with him. But then there is this gift called grace which comes with no strings attached, and which cannot be earned. You take it or leave it. Pouring through the firmament as it does, it should be inescapable, though some people manage to do without it. When Jesus met those who knew nothing about grace he told them, 'Come unto me all you who are burdened with worries and pains, and all the back-breaking business of living, and I will refresh you.'

Grace is the gift of renewal, of refreshment. It flows from that transfigured Jesus. When Peter, James and John received it in abundance on Mount Hermon they said, 'It is good, Lord, to be here.'

In Isaiah's shocking picture of the rejected Messiah we have a description of our soiling the face of God. It fills us with horror: 'He hath no form nor comeliness; and when we see him, there is no beauty that we should desire him. He is despised and rejected of men; a man of sorrows, and acquainted with grief; and we hid as it were our faces from him.'

At the Transfiguration we, like his friends, again hide our faces from him, though for a very different reason, he the radiant one, we knowing what we are. For them the teacher, alongside whom they had trod the dusty roads, slept in the open air, shared their food, was now a blinding light. So near to him now were they that they could hear his Father's voice. It terrified them. But he walked over to where they fell, touched their trembling bodies and said, 'Don't be afraid.' Once on their feet they 'saw Jesus only'. It entitles us to ask, 'What is a vision?' A vision is the experience of a special recognition of God. Sometimes what is heard is as important as what is seen. Peter, James and John both saw and heard God because 'they saw Jesus only'. We read of poor old Eli, a priest 'who was never granted the vision'.

Mercifully, no weakness, nor corruption even, can prevent us from seeing Jesus only. Our sight of him may be bleared by the defects in our nature, though never sufficiently to totally obscure him. We may not be fit to stand with him on the mountain-top, but that in a sense is our choice. They were all four of them at prayer when the Transfiguration happened. It was something they did every day – prayed together. Although now and then *he* went off to pray alone. As Jews, the disciples possessed an advantage over us Gentiles, for they would have known of another transfiguration, that of their great leader Moses whose face so shone after talking to God on Mount Sinai that he had to wear a veil when he descended. Seeing the shining Jesus, unveiled, glorious to behold, they knew that they themselves would now have to go from splendour to splendour, as St Paul said.

When we were children we were taught a simple hymn which ran, 'Jesus bids us shine with a pure clear light'. It could have been our first step up Mount Hermon. People come to Mount Bures to climb our Mount, all thirty-five feet of it. It is August and when we open the church windows wide maybe they will hear our Transfiguration hymn.

> 'Tis good, Lord, to be here!
> Yet we may not remain;
> But since thou bidst us leave the mount
> Come with us to the plain.

The Passport to the Kingdom

---◆---

One of Christ's most provocative sayings is that in order to enter his Kingdom we must become a child. 'Like this child here', he demonstrated, taking a little boy up in his arms. Three of the Gospels record him insisting on this condition for entry. Close friends found it impossible. Impossible too was it for them to keep their natural ambitions out of discipleship. Had they not given up everything to obey another of his orders – 'Follow me'? Gone were family life, home, jobs and respectability. They had become vagabonds like him. Now and then the authorities harried them. Always they had their eye on them. Life was certainly exciting and, they supposed, rewarding, but it was not easy. It rarely is if one is a disciple. To be a disciple one has to follow a teacher. Jesus's disciples were learning some things fast and some things not at all. Such as having to be a child once more in order to gain admittance to his 'kingdom'. It was the opposite to what was usual. Teachers showed one how to grow up, how to be adult, to mature. The world needed maturity. Leaders offered their helpers portfolios when they came into power.

The mother of two of the disciples spoke up for her sons.

'My Lord, when you come into your Kingdom will you seat them at your right and left hand?'

Jesus sighed. She still had not grasped – none of them had – what his Kingdom was, what it meant. Such places, he said, were not in his gift.

It was the word 'kingdom' which muddled them. They all knew what a king was and what a king did. He reigned, he appointed. Now this extraordinary person was telling them that, although a king, he could not appoint. Why could they not enter his Kingdom except as children? Did he mean as innocents? They were full grown, how could they be innocent?

> At the same time came the disciples unto Jesus, saying, Who is the greatest in the kingdom of heaven? And Jesus called a little child unto him, and set him in the midst of them, and said, Verily I say unto you, except ye be converted, and become as little children, ye shall not enter into the kingdom of heaven. Whosoever therefore shall humble himself as this little child, the same is greatest in the kingdom of heaven.
>
> (Matthew 18.1–4, KJV)

He had lost them again. I always think that it is one of the strengths of the New Testament that it takes bewilderment into account. Over and over again we have puzzled faces, blank faces. Repeatedly, we have the Gospel writers recording the disciples' inability to follow Jesus, not on the road but in his statements. And now he is saying that even a child can follow his meaning. It is a reproach. There were those who spoke back. How could a man or woman become a child – be reborn? Oh, sure, who would not like to have a second chance, a second go at life! 'If I knew then what I know now . . .' The philosopher-poet Omar Khayyam put this rueful thought in the language of pottery:

> Ah, love, could'st thou and I with fate conspire
> To shape this crooked state of things entire,
> Would we not shatter it to bits – and then
> Re-mould it nearer to our heart's desire?

However, what's done cannot be undone, and all that we can hope for is God's forgiveness and God's praise.

Jesus does not think like this. He thinks in terms of regeneration and renewal. He tells his friends about God's grace. There it is, filling the universe. Good conduct, even saintly conduct, cannot earn it. It has to be there for the taking by the worst and the best of us, grace, God's grace streaming through the firmament. There it is, you have it for the asking or you can say, no thank you. Not today.

Christ's most intriguing conversation about the Kingdom is with the most furtive of his disciples, a man named Nicodemus. It takes place in the city of Capernaum and at night. Nicodemus was not a poor homesick fisherman who must at times have longed far more for his cottage by the lakeside than for this 'kingdom' which was being promised him. Nicodemus was a member of the High Council and a person of importance. But he was secretly enthralled by Jesus and he had reached the position where he had to accept that someone who wrought miracles was no ordinary man. Eventually the day – or rather the night – came when he had to have it out with this strange person. Who *was* Jesus? What was he actually saying? And thus, muffled up to the eyes and slipping through back lanes, he reached the Lord's house. How embarrassing if someone he knew saw him. 'Hallo, Lord Nicodemus, where on earth are you off to at this time of night?' How dangerous. An elected member of the High Council consulting a notorious itinerant preacher! But his reason for doing so was sensible enough. If a man can do miracles for other people, then God must be with him.

Jesus brushes away this polite reason for Nicodemus's visit. He knows the truth about this caller. He gets down to hard facts. He is like a doctor telling a patient what he has to do. 'I tell you truthfully that unless you are reborn you will never enter the Kingdom.'

Nicodemus takes this literally. How can he re-enter the womb? It is absurd.

Jesus sees that although he is talking to an important person, he is also a childish person. 'You have to be born of water – undergo baptism. You have to be born of the spirit. Be sensible. That which is born physically is physical. That which is born spiritually is spiritual. So do not find it impossible to believe when I tell you, "You must be born again."'

He continues, like a poet, 'The wind blows where it likes and you can hear it, but you cannot tell where it begins or where it ends.' Not everything can be explained.

The visitor is far from convinced even by this. 'How? What are you telling me?'

Jesus says, 'Are you not one of our appointed authorities, and you don't understand what I am saying? If you cannot believe in my earthly message as it is revealed in my actions among the sick and the poor, what hope is there of your comprehending my "Kingdom"?' And then it is to Nicodemus alone that Christ utters those marvellous words, 'For God so loved the world, that he gave his only begotten Son, that whosoever believes in him should not die, but have everlasting life.'

We hear of Nicodemus only once more. It is when he brings to the tomb a hundredweight of spices to embalm the mangled body who had told him that God loved the world so much that he would die for it. Such a funerary gesture was far from furtive. It branded Councillor Nicodemus a follower. Did he care? His action says that he did not.

I was listening to Nicholas Tolstoi on the radio the other day. He was talking about the dual strands of Christianity, one mysterious, one practical. He said that all great faiths are about earth and about what we call 'heaven'. There are the kingdoms of the world and there is the Kingdom of God. The Christian leads his earthly life so that he can every now and then catch a glimpse of the everlasting, of the eternal.

He tries to put aside every now and then some of his grown-upness and be Christ's child. Tolstoi said that his own experience of 'heaven' came through the incomparable liturgy of the Russian Orthodox Church, which is its intention. In the village church where I often preach there are two kinds of window, that filled with clear glass and that with painted glass. In heavenly terms both have to be looked through, not *at*. Through the clear glass we glimpse nature – a cloud, a yew, a passing bird. Through the coloured glass we glimpse other worlds than this. In Herbert's words,

> A man that looks on glasse,
>   On it may stay his eye;
> Or, if he pleaseth, through it pass,
>   And then the heav'n espie.

English stained glass and Russian icons once served the same purpose. The gaze travelled through their imagery to discover the real. Nicholas Tolstoi said that Christianity has to be something more than a moral system, more than a set of laws. It was because Jesus taught this that he was executed. His insistence on there being an altogether greater law, that of love, unqualified love, was an alarming idea for 'religion' to accept. His kingdom was simply where love reigned. To enter it meant to unload all the clutter we have acquired through being unloving and unlovely, and to be as we were. As a child, he suggested. A tall order, we say. His friends shooed the children away from the often weary figure. But as they were the perfect object lesson for his grown-up followers he said, 'Let them come to me for of such is the kingdom of heaven.'

The Necessity of the Psalm

Leaving a great cathedral, drifting towards its sunlit door, I told the person near to me how I had especially loved the psalm. It was the one in which the psalmist calls his tongue 'the pen of a ready writer' (Psalm 45).

She said, 'We do not have the psalms in our church.'

'Never?'

'Never.'

I could not believe it. I had no idea that there were parish churches which did not sing psalms. For how can we follow the teachings of Christ and ignore the fact that they constantly reveal his familiarity with the psalms? They were his hymnbook and he and all his people drew from them the right words for whatever befell them, terrible experiences or blissful experiences. Here are the best words for the heights or the depths. The Lord sang them at the Last Supper and found them in his mouth during the crises of his life. Once he heard the Tempter quote them – 'He shall give his angels charge over thee' (Psalm 91). If in Christ's speech, so in ours. Their phrases are part of our common language. 'Out of the mouths of babes and sucklings . . . Keep me as the apple of an eye . . . Oh that I had wings like a dove . . .

Aldhelmsburgh

For a thousand years in thy sight are but as yesterday . . . The days of our age are three score years and ten.'

A 'psalm' is a poem sung to the accompaniment of an instrument: in David's day a harp, in George Herbert's case to his lute, in ours to the organ. At Mount Bures we say them, myself one verse, the little congregation the next, and very satisfying it is, the beautiful familiar words falling rhythmically in the ancient nave. I almost prefer this to the magnificent settings at Westminster Abbey where the music is too advanced for congregational participation and the choir too glorious. But never for one moment do I not remember that whatever psalm it is, and how ever uttered, it was heard in the Temple by Jesus and his forebears. The influence of this divine Jewish song on our lives, our literature and our liturgy is incalculable. Nothing is as consoling, nothing as ecstatic, few writings as wise. It was through this old hymnbook that the Jewish nation was able to release its soul to the Gentiles, and to translate Palestine to Wales or Italy or Suffolk, or wherever. Those dancing hills, those benign valleys, those slimy depths, that arid waste, those trees, that pelican, bear an easy transition to any native landscape.

And of course the psalms are the chief route to the Christian hymnal. During the centuries when the priests held on to the Bible, fearing the laity's myriad interpretations, the Book of Psalms alone was allowed to the people to read. It became precious to them. They found it especially useful on death, and the brevity of earthly life generally. It calmed their natural fears. Owen Chadwick said that when Thomas Sternhold and John Hopkins published a metrical version of the Psalms in 1547 it taught the people of England and Scotland more about the Christian religion than any other book, except, of course, the New Testament itself. A century or so later George Herbert rhymed the Twenty-third Psalm to perfection. Sternhold and Hopkins's Psalter was eventually republished by John Day of Dunwich, 'printer to the Reformation'. Those hymns which are pre-fixed 'old' – as the Old Hundredth – come from this book.

In the Psalms the countryside is both lovely and practical, sacred and workaday. It is a land which is full of common sense but at the same time intoxicatingly imaginative. It is full of sheep and corn and refreshing streams – and dangers! Animals dwell in it with much happiness and are sometimes gentle and sometimes terrible. 'The fir-trees are a dwelling for the stork. The high hills are a refuge for the wild goats: and so are the stony rocks for the conies.' If one word could sum up the philosophy of the psalmist it would be 'refuge'. Man and beast find their rightful place in it and are protected by their Creator. And he shares their natural habitat, arriving in it 'like rain into a fleece of wool'.

But all is not good, all is not welcome. There are these horrible pits, these dark waters and, worst of all, this valley of the shadow of death to which all must come. It is at this point of the journey that the psalm reaches its height of protection and reassurance. The God of the Psalms is a protector-God and a parent-God who draws from his mortal children their joyous dependency. 'I will give thanks unto thee, O Lord, with my whole heart . . . I will praise thy name because of thy loving-kindness and truth.' This parent-God is inescapable. 'If I climb up into heaven, thou art there: if I go down to hell, thou art there also. If I take the wings of the morning and remain in the uttermost parts of the sea – even there shall thy hand hold me.'

Now and then the psalmist is impatient with old tunes and words – 'O sing unto the Lord a *new* song – let the congregation of saints praise him.' We in our village churches are a congregation of saints in biblical language and as such 'the Lord has pleasure in us'. We give him pleasure in return and he gives us all that we possess. 'So let us praise his name in the dance.' Such phrases remind us that the Psalms are Eastern music and passionate and wild at times. They alternate between earthiness and grandeur. From God giving fodder to cattle to the God 'who maketh his angels spirits and his ministers a flaming fire'. In them the Lord is our light, our strength, our Redeemer, our everyday friend, 'our never failing help in time of trouble'.

All words, you might say. But such words! Words which men and women have lived by for upwards of three thousand years. Words which Christ knew by heart and frequently quoted. Words which we still fly to when we are in big trouble and ill – and which we should fly to when we are trouble-free and well. Early in the Christian era poets and musicians began to supplement this ancient hymnbook with new numbers, so to speak. In the fourth century a writer almost as inspired as the psalmist himself appeared, Ambrose, Bishop of Milan and close friend of St Augustine. It was St Ambrose who insisted that the whole congregation should sing, and not just the choir. It was he who stressed the need of morning and evening song:

> To thee our morning song of praise,
> To thee our evening prayer we raise.

God hears humanity calling him in the Psalms, calling him urgently, calling him eloquently, and we, singing them Sunday after Sunday, are conscious of joining in this calling. Jesus would often have sat on the Temple steps listening to the Temple choir and hearing words which we know.

> Be still, and know that I am God: I will be exalted among the heathen, I will be exalted in the earth. The Lord of hosts is with us; the God of Jacob is our refuge.
>
> (Psalm 46.10–11, KJV)

The Brother Slave

——⋅◆⋅——

People often ring up to ask what lesson they have to read. To one caller I answered, 'Philemon'. '*All* of it?' All of it. All of it is just a few lines from Paul, just a few paragraphs. It is the only private letter of his that has come down to us. All the rest of his letters are public ones, written to various churches in Asia Minor and to great Rome itself. But when he wrote briefly to Philemon it was to beg him – not order him – to conduct himself in a quite extraordinary manner with regard to a runaway slave. It is not at all the customary plea for leniency and instead of concerning itself with what might legally happen to his slave, it puts the owner on the spot. It is the kind of letter which threatens havoc to a God-fearing house, turning its conventions upside down. We can imagine Philemon passing it over to this wife and muttering, 'Well!' The fact that theirs was no ordinary house, but a house-church, would only have added to the discomfiture.

Paul has written to his old friend Philemon from his Roman prison to tell him that his slave Onesimus – 'Profitable' – has made his way there from distant Asia Minor and that he has converted him and made him his son, therefore all the previous relationships have changed, for this is what happens to Christians. As Paul's son the slave must become his owner's brother, and since one cannot enslave a brother, Onesimus will have to be freed. Had he not been your property, I would have kept him here, as he has been a great help to me, says Paul. Adding, and probably thinking about Onesimus's name – 'Profitable' – should you be out of pocket about all this, don't worry, I will pay.

Slavery was the norm in the Roman empire and in Colossae where Philemon and Apphia (his wife?) ran their house-church. It was a beautiful Phrygian city on the banks of the River Lycus. Paul was having some trouble with the Colossians due to their holding on to earlier religious philosophies and mixing them with the gospel of Christ. And no wonder, for this city was on the great trading route from Ephesus to the Euphrates on which news of every kind travelled fast. He would have seen the lettered slaves teaching in the schools and the unlettered ones toiling in the fields or mending the roads. Wherever he and Timothy stopped for a bed or for a meal, in inns or private houses – or a house-church – a slave would have at once moved forward to remove their sandals and wash their dirty feet, the lowliest of tasks. When Jesus did likewise, reversing the role, his friends were appalled and embarrassed.

It was just as they were about to sit down and eat what would be their last supper together before whatever dreadful fate it was struck their beloved Master. Although John said that it was 'to show the full extent of his love', it was too much for Peter, who drew back.

'I will never let you wash *my* feet!'

'If I don't we cannot be friends.'

'Then, Lord, not only my feet but head, hands too.'

'You are clean all over.'

It took Peter some time to be both slave and apostle, as Christ was both servant and king. It is poignant to realize that Jesus would have washed the feet of Judas and dried them with the towel he had tucked round his waist. In some of the paintings of the Last Supper clean, bare feet are prominent below the table, feet which would soon be tramping the Emmaus road or the world.

Onesimus's feet would have been sore when he got to Rome. Although we are not told his age, he sounds young. He sounds as if his master's friend Paul made a tremendous impression on him and gave him the strength to run away. By managing to reach Paul he had in effect changed masters. Paul may have said amazing things in the house-church, such as there being neither master nor servant, only free men, perfected men – just men. All the same, by Philemon's standards Onesimus had done the worst thing a slave could do. He had run away. Runaway slaves were severely punished. They were unprofitable, difficult to resell and some of their owners preferred them to be a dead loss. Paul knew what could happen to Onesimus, house-church or no house-church. The slave-trade being so profitable, it would take the followers of the servant-King nineteen hundred years to abolish slavery. Onesimus is one of the first slaves to be owned by a Christian. Paul's letter is so graphic, so excellently put that it should have nipped Christian slavery in the bud, but alas it did not. He wrote:

> I might make bold to point out your duty . . . Yes, I, Paul, ambassador as I am of Christ Jesus – and now his prisoner – appeal to you about *my child*, whose father I have become in this prison. I mean Onesimus, once so little use to you, but now useful indeed, to both you and me. I am sending him back to you, and in doing so I am sending part of myself. I should have liked to keep him with me, to look after me as you would wish, here in prison for the gospel. But I would rather do nothing without your consent, so that your kindness may be a matter not of compulsion, but of your own free will. For perhaps this is why you lost him for a time, that you might have him back for good, *no longer as a slave, but . . . as a dear brother*, very dear indeed to me and how much dearer to you, both as man and as Christian. If, then, you count me your partner in the faith, *welcome him as you would welcome me.* And if he has done you any wrong or is in your debt put that down to my account. Here is my signature, PAUL; I will repay . . . Now brother, as a Christian, be generous with me, and relieve my anxiety; we are both in Christ!

(Philemon 8, 9–20, NEB)

And he ends his upsetting letter with, 'Have a room ready for me, for I hope that in answer to your prayers God will let me come to you.' Alas, poor old man, he would never retrace his steps to Colossae. The emperor whose earthly subject he was – and had been proud to be – was Nero. Paul had dictated the letter to Philemon to Onesimus himself, and may have enclosed it in his Letter to the Colossians.

What happened to the runaway slave whom Paul had made his son we have no way of finding out. But both Philemon and Onesimus could not escape the mutual freedom given them by the servant-King, and this they would have known. Wilberforce and all those who fought against the profitability of the slave-trade would have read Philemon.

In his Revelation St John has a vision of the destruction of materialism. He sees what he calls 'the merchants of these things' mourning because everything they had set their hearts on had crashed. He lists their merchandise and it includes 'slaves, and souls of men'.

There are still vast numbers of slaves in the world, and those who are as good as slaves. Men, women and children ticketed 'Profitable' who, like Onesimus, can be bought and sold on market-day. Paul's letter should have stopped the bidding long ago.

A Letter from Paul

At breakfast one person receives a letter and may out of kindness dole out a sentence or two from it for the rest of us. But the person to whom the letter is addressed reads on and on, giving a little laugh, a big sigh, a gasp of amazement, skips a page, looks pleased, looks disturbed. When the letter comes to an end the recipient tells us that the writer sends us love, though no news, of course. The news in the letter is not for us. The letter will have cast a mood, a spell. The receiver of the letter is not quite as she was before it arrived. She now knows something which we do not know. All the same, though mightily curious, should the letter be left on the table we will not read it. Or rather I would not – but I had a friend who did read other people's letters without shame.

Paul told the church at Galatia, 'You see how large a letter I have written unto you with mine own hand!' He said this because he often dictated his letters to one of his young assistants, Timothy or Luke. Galatians is indeed a large letter. Paul wrote it in Rome where news had come to him that the church there had reverted to Jewish laws and customs which excluded Gentiles, and he calls them 'foolish

Galatians!' as he rams home the universality of Christ. It is of no consequence whether a Christian is Jewish or Greek or black or white or clever or dim or great or humble, and he reminds them in this large letter written in his own hand of his authority as an apostle. This remarkable letter was written with an unusual, passionate intensity and the Galatians must have been overwhelmed by it. They would certainly not have been as they were before it arrived.

Paul's letter to the Philippians was taken down by Epaphroditus whom he calls 'brother and fellow-soldier', and that to the Colossians by two fellow-soldiers, Tychicus and Onesimus. Tychicus became a bishop, Onesimus was a literate slave whom Paul set free. A young man named Tertius was the secretary who took down one of the most influential letters ever written, that of St Paul to the Romans. He called the Roman Christians 'the saints of Caesar's household'. It was to them that he emphasized the world-wide nature of the faith, for at that moment the Jews were being expelled from Rome and he was anxious that the new Church should not be thought of as a Jewish sect.

So many of Paul's letters were written in prison that I sometimes wonder if they were the only places where an enforced idleness made it possible for him *to* write. They belong to the great library of prison-writing in which are found all kinds of literary masterpieces, many of which would not have got on to the page had their authors not been behind bars. Paul wrote to the Romans while he was still free at Corinth, sending his letter by 'Phoebe, servant of the church at Cenchrea'. After the famous attack on Roman morals it opens out into a marvellously eloquent and persuasive account of the complete life which can be had in Christ. If there was much to be given up, there was even more to compensate. The city was a wild place where the celebrated Roman peace was kept by means of brutal entertainments. Paul had to show it something even more captivating. He calls it 'the splendour of the divine', using the phrase a number of times. By faith they – we – will move into the splendour of the divine. Roman empire glories – how can they be compared with the glory of the Kingdom? That place where, as the old hymn puts it, 'I through grace a member am'? He tells the Romans to hold on to their individualism. They are not to be busybodies where each other's Christianity is concerned. It takes all sorts to make a Church.

Death is in the air, death to make amusement and spectacle. Tertius, writing the following down, would have shivered. Or maybe have sat upright, full of new purpose. 'For none of us liveth to himself, and no man dieth to himself. For whether we live, we live unto the Lord; and whether we die, we die unto the Lord: whether we live therefore, or die, we are the Lord's.'

And then, as in so many of Paul's letters, he signs off with a list of names, anxious not to leave anyone out, and sending his love to Priscilla, Aquila, Mary, Andronicus, Junia,

Urbane, Apeles, Narcissus, Rufus 'and his mother and mine', Hermes, Julia, Olympas . . . taking us all into the original congregation of the Holy City, and allowing Tertius the scribe to add his love too. There are many women's names. Paul is frequently reviled as anti-feminist, and yet come to the closing sentences of his letters, and what do we find? Women like Phoebe holding important office in the Church, women like Tryphena and Tryphosa 'who toil in the Lord's service', women who are clearly ministering to house-churches. It is the later male element in the Church which glossed over these 'first ladies' of the Christian era who were so essential to its foundation.

My favourite conversion by the dramatically converted Paul is that of St Augustine. Three and a half centuries have passed since the letters were written and for scholars like Augustine they are 'literature'. In August 386, when he was thirty-two, and had been searching this way and that for God and the meaning of life, and was in an emotional turmoil about becoming a Christian, he heard over the garden wall a child's voice repeating the refrain 'Take it and read, take it and read'. He could not tell whether it was the voice of a boy or a girl and at first thought it was one of those chanting games which children play on their own. 'Take it and read, take it and read.' He then recalled that a friend of his had wandered into a church while the gospel was being read, and because he thought it was being addressed to him personally, *had* been converted. 'Take it and read, take it and read,' sang the boy or girl over the garden wall. St Paul's Letters lay nearby. He opened the book at Romans 13 and began the passage which centuries later would be read throughout Advent:

> The night is far spent, the day is at hand: let us therefore cast off the works of darkness, and let us put on the armour of light. Let us walk honestly, as in the day; not in rioting and drunkenness, not in chambering and wantonness, not in strife and envying. But put ye on the Lord Jesus Christ, and make not provision for the flesh to fulfil the lusts thereof.
>
> (Romans 13.12–14 RJV)

Augustine, soon to be St Augustine, marked the place and went into the house to tell his mother that he was now a Christian. No doubt the child went on playing. What comes from the mouths of babes and sucklings is often monotonous, and presumably aimless where they themselves are concerned.

A Career Wife

The proverbially perfect and all-round woman is found in – Proverbs. King Lemuel's description of her is based on what his mother taught him. A wife has to be an all-rounder, a busy and accomplished person who works day and night. The woman who the King's mother has in mind runs a big domestic establishment, a farm and a linen business. She is none other than that famous woman who is, in the words of Solomon, 'above rubies'. This woman is no mere housewife, if any housewife can be called mere. She is a woman of the world as well as of the hearth. She runs her husband's empire as he is away a great deal, politicking presumably, leaving much for his wife to do. She is, we are told, like a fleet of merchant ships bringing food from afar, an image which today translates into a laden supermarket trolley. She buys a field and plants a vineyard in it. She is physically strong. She goes to bed late and gets up when it is still dark and, all in all, she is a paragon.

The woman who is above rubies is also above fashion because 'strength and honour are her clothing'. She is a statesman's dream-wife, someone he can leave everything to, someone who will never two-time him, spend all his money or bring sloth or scandal into his life. She is also what previous generations would term 'a lady', someone with presence and status. It is not only the Roman officer who orders his man to 'do that and he doeth it'. The woman of business and affairs has her own command.

In the past many young women would have been told to emulate the woman who was above rubies, who is privileged but also good, using her position and money to everybody's benefit. But she would have been a grimly materialistic woman had she not 'feared the Lord'. When we hear of Bible characters 'fearing' God it does not mean that they were in dread of him or that he frightened them. To 'fear' the Lord meant to revere him, to show him reverence. The clergy are approached reverentially, not fearfully – at least one hopes not. The reverence towards God was the key to the character of the woman who was above rubies.

With some drastic updating, what we have in this woman is a 'type' of the twenty-first century's wife who runs a house, a family and a department. A woman bustling about getting the dinner ready was once too much for Jesus. Mary listened and was still, paying attention to what he said. Martha could not be still because she was cooking, laying the table, listening to all those sounds which told her what was done, what needed a few more minutes. She had her favourite guest, the beloved young rabbi. It must have wounded her to get the rough edge of his tongue. In the sanctuary window of our old church there is a Victorian picture of the two sisters, Mary very still and entranced by what she was hearing, Martha staggering in with a pile of plates. Mary has a halo but Martha has not – which I have always thought unfair. A woman as close to Christ as Martha was holy enough for a halo.

But of course her Lord was right. Throughout the ages there are women who have been too busy to listen, to read, to be still, acquiring wealth and status and clothes and 'pleasure', talking and cleaning and shopping and packing in a good day at the office. Christ sees such women as he saw the jolly farmer who had the heart attack just when he was about to enjoy his good harvest, or the young man who had everything but who could not see that his money was, for him, a barrier against his spiritual fulfilment. We criticize Jesus at times for his 'unworldliness', for saying drastic things such as 'Let the dead bury the dead' or 'Give away all you have and follow me' – or 'Let the dinner burn when I am speaking'. Yet we know that, harsh though these commands are, they do embody great truths regarding our happiness here on earth as well as our spiritual fulfilment. He is reminding us how finite we are. And in our day how we trivialize our one and only life on a lovely planet by so many obsessions, domestic, financial, fashionable, etc. We know perfectly well what he is getting at! His words are warning words. 'Lay not up for yourselves earthly treasure, lay up spiritual resources, for without these you will be poor however much is in the bank.' He is speaking about investments.

So cleverly structured are we these days in the other kind of investment that we find Christ's attitudes irresponsible. His rules are apt to run flat in the face of our rules. Young people are at this very moment being advised by government to save for the morrow, the 'morrow' being their old age. The old, when they were young, were made by government to provide for their morrow, only to discover that this provision goes hardly anywhere, and so both young and old are preoccupied with pensions. Neither regard them as earthly treasure. Every generation, from his day to our own, attempts some kind of providence and the anti-materialism of religion is seen as a check on greed and grab, money-obsession and a kind of impossible ideal. The rich only manage to scrape into heaven.

The woman who was above rubies would have been a workaholic straight out of Dickens's *Hard Times* had she not 'feared the Lord'. Her tale, as told in Proverbs, ends with, 'Give her of the fruit of her hands and let her own works praise her in the gates'. What does this mean? Well, at the beginning of this remarkable woman's biography we learn that her husband has a high position among the rulers of the land who meet at the gates of the city, and that his wife is known there as a power in her own right. She it is whose linen manufactory, etc., helps to provide the funds for his career. It is an extraordinary tale about a female entrepreneur supporting her husband's profession. Were it not for the fact that she combined this with a deep sense of dependency upon her God, and with common sense and kindness towards everyone with whom she came into daily contact, using her money for the social good, she would not have been valued above rubies. There is an American joke. 'How much did he leave?' 'He left it all.' The business-woman in Proverbs left the world a better place. But so too did Martha. She fed the homeless Teacher.

The Singer of
Sad Songs

———◆———

A captured people, far from home, is brought news of that home. It was a beautiful home, none other than legendary Jerusalem, the city of cities. And it had been systematically destroyed by its conquerors. We ourselves have seen such deliberate destruction and as a nation have been guilty of it.

'On the fifth day of the tenth month in the twelfth year of our captivity, fugitives came to me from Jerusalem and told me that the city had fallen.'

The speaker is a young prisoner named Jeremiah. He could have added, 'I told you so!' Had he not gone about Jerusalem warning both people and government what would happen if they did not mend their ways – and their defences? But nobody had listened to him. It was the beginning of his reputation for being a prophet of doom. We still say, do we not, 'Oh, don't be a Jeremiah, don't be such a pessimist, don't be such a prophet of doom!' But Jeremiah was none of these things. He was a man of warning and had his country listened to him it would not have been captured.

'Man, your fellow-countrymen gather in groups and talk of you under walls, and in doorways, and say to one another, "Let us go and see what the message is from the Lord." So my people will come crowding in, as people do, and sit down in front of you. They will hear what you have to say, but they will not do it! "Fine words!" they will say.'

We can hear Jeremiah's exasperation all these centuries hence. Dreadful unnecessary things have occurred in our lifetime simply because some leader or other has not taken the best advice. Jeremiah was told that his people were too busy making profits to be bothered by a prophet. 'Why,' they told him to his face, 'you are no more to them than a singer of fine songs with a lovely voice.' He does indeed have a lovely voice. The Book of Jeremiah is among the most ravishing pages of the Bible, and full of poetry.

What was happening in his country to make Jeremiah write such a book? Was there not a promising young king on the throne? Was there not a comfortable life for a great many of his subjects and food enough for everyone and to spare? Was not God in his holy box in the Temple, safe and sound? To celebrate this dwelling of God in the midst of his chosen people, glorious liturgies were sung antiphonally all day long. The bad times were over. The nation could now pursue worship and art and all civilized matters. Who would dream of harming such a holy city? A small country with a mighty city set between two rivers would – Babylon.

This fairly distant land was expansionist and Judah was

on its list. It seems that only Jeremiah realized this. Everyone else was keen to put such threats out of their minds. Babylon too has a new king. His name is Nebuchadnezzar and his father it was who had founded the Babylonian empire. Sons like to build on to family empires, and there, not all that far away, and barely protected from predators such as he, was this enchanting land named Judah with its famous teachers and fabulous Temple filled, it was said, with gold and jewels. Nebuchadnezzar wants Jerusalem for two reasons, its treasure and its clever men and their families. The Temple plate would be something out of this world for his banquets and the Jews would improve the Babylonian stock. And so the King of Babylon would deport a nation, leaving behind a demoralized remnant as a kind of caretaker of ruin. It seemed to him a novel form of empire expansion, un-bloodthirsty and in its way, civilized. He was manic, of course, and would become mad.

The young man who foresaw this tragedy could not have been more sane. Although God's communications with him came via dreams, when Jeremiah spoke it was as the most clear-headed realist. There are such people in every age and if only governments acted on their commonsense advice many of the disasters of history would never have happened. There were those who saw the First World War looming when everyone else said, 'Impossible!' Europe's Jews themselves during the early 1930s could not believe that tenders were being put in by governments for the means to rid

Europe of them once and for all. But Jeremiah says, and what he says must always be in the present tense, 'Nothing is too mad or too wicked for a nation to do.'

When nobody would listen to his spoken words, Jeremiah decided to write his warnings down, dictating them to Baruch, a man who could carry them to the king himself. 'And Baruch wrote from the mouth of Jeremiah all the words of the Lord which he had spoken unto him, upon a roll of a book.' You will remember that when Jesus read the lesson at Nazareth he did so from the roll of the prophet Isaiah. Such rolls are in use in synagogues today. First Baruch read Jeremiah's book to the High Court, then to the people at the city gate, then to all the princes, and they said, 'It must be read to the King!'

It was winter and the King was sitting by the fire in his palace. 'Read the roll to me,' he ordered a scribe.

As he heard what fate had in store for him, and as Jeremiah's book unrolled, he cut off the pieces which had been read with a penknife and threw them in the fire. He was doing what men have always done to books which offend them. Think of the bishops burning William Tyndale's Bible and the Nazis making bonfires of non-Aryan literature. It is a strangely up-to-date scene in King Jehoiakim's palace on that wintry day, with him bit by bit feeding the flames with Jeremiah's words. I have always been fascinated by the circumstantial detail – the dictation, the penknife, the brazier.

No writer did more than Jeremiah to get his book read. It was God who had dictated it to him – and the beautiful language in which he wrote was certainly a gift from above. Alas, it was the latter which caused people not to take him too seriously. He was 'no more than a singer of fine songs with a lovely voice'. More attention would have been given to his prophecies had they been written in the style of a government White Paper. And, anyway, it was usual for young men to be world-changing and enthusiastic. To be fair to the religious establishment in Jerusalem, it recognized that there had to be change and more up-to-date ideas were being introduced. But Jeremiah saw these reforms as no more than a patching-up of worn-out beliefs. What he wanted was a full-scale return to God. Nothing less could avert the total destruction of Jerusalem. When his book went unread, he said that he might just as well have tied a stone to it and thrown it into the river.

In it he writes some words – 'All is well, all well? Nothing is well' – which bring to mind another author, Julian of Norwich. But she is an optimist. The world was in a frightful state in her day but she could say, 'All shall be well, and all shall be well, and all manner of things shall be well.' Her optimism stemmed from her belief in Christ's ultimate victory.

Jeremiah was convinced of Nebuchadnezzar's ultimate victory if God was not put in full charge of Jerusalem. When the Babylonian army arrived it took the holy city easily and burnt it to the ground. All its scholars and craftsmen were taken into captivity, all its sacred works of art were looted. Centuries later another sad and eloquent young man would gaze across the beloved city. It was the Christ.

> And when he was come near, he beheld the city, and wept over it, saying, If thou hadst known, even thou, at least in this thy day, the things which belong unto thy peace! But now they are hid from thine eyes. For the days shall come upon thee, that thine enemies shall cast a trench about thee, and compass thee round . . . and they shall not leave in thee one stone upon another.
>
> (Luke 19.41–3, KJV)

Jesus knew Jeremiah's book, not just as a book of warning but also as a book of promises. The promises come in chapter 30 and they include, 'You shall be my people, and I will be your God'. Christians have always used the captivity of Israel as a lesson about being far from home, about being aliens in this world. We now rightly believe that both earth and heaven are 'home' to us. The lament of Jeremiah and his countrymen is that of every exile to this day. The singer of fine songs now catches the ear of many nations.

Combined Truths:
the Harvest at Wormingford

---◆---

Both the Jewish and Christian faiths overflow with harvests, as do all religions since many of them grew out of farming practice. Deuteronomy, the book which Christ so frequently quoted, commands the Israelites to celebrate harvests. They were to bring samples of their best corn, fruit and stock to the altar and to thank God for their fields and pastures. This 'harvest-home' was called the Feast of Tabernacles, the 'tabernacles' being the temporary huts they lived in on the cleared land to remind them of their wanderings, and to remind them too that they were now home. Close to them was the acacia wood box containing God's law and round it was spread all the wealth which a settled community could produce, wheat, fruit, oil, wine, wool, water from the local well, honey. We can imagine the beautiful scene, the Transjordanian fields all cut, the orchards picked, the singing in the open air. And to be realistic, the calloused hands and aching backs, not to mention the sighs of relief if it was a good harvest and the anxious faces if it was not. These ancient people, unlike us, had three harvest festivals each year, three ingatherings, but the feast of Tabernacles was the greatest. It was at the time of this feast that Christ would tell his followers that he had come to renew the law which lay at the centre of all their prosperity, not to abolish it.

When we read the Bible we are reading about local happenings, about rural people, about having to put something into the ground (or life) before getting something out, and about gratitude. Our own harvest festival has to be a feast of gratitude spread before the giver of all things. We do not have to set aside our dealings in today's markets, with their computers and agri-science, and regress to sheaves and binders in order to acknowledge this gratitude. What is important is that we continue to think of what happens at this time of the year in and around Wormingford as harvest, and not simply 'business'. When I take the twists and turns of the lanes to the river, I constantly think of the farming feet which made them. Some of us took part in the final horse harvests, ourselves and half the village in the field. An increasing number of us no longer see fields, only the traffic running between them. What went on in them for centuries, all that skill, all that custom, is now explained away in the theme park. It is becoming quite a struggle to prevent everything which existed here until forty or so years ago from sliding into the leisure industry.

On the very spot where we now worship many thousands of men and women accepted the cycle of farming which

Harvest Festival 1930 (detail)
The church is Draycot Ceme, Wiltshire

bound their temporal and eternal concepts of life together. Whether by road or footpath, I do not often go to church without being aware of other feet going that way. Not ghostly feet, but ordinary country feet stamping their destinations – never very far – on the landscape. Market-day at Colchester or Sudbury, otherwise most days on the land. 'He or she worked on the land.' That is what they said. It told one everything. What we have quite forgotten in the village is the old uproar. The carrying talk of working groups, the shouts of many children by the river, garden conversation, bouts of singing in the pub or forge, and the clatter and buzz of the farmyard. Villages were noisy in the late summer due to everyone being outside. Among its quietest occupations were blackberrying, sloe-ing, mushrooming, fishing – and courting. But the little sounds which these made would seem strangely noisy to us, accustomed as we are to a place where scarcely a voice is heard.

Harvest Festival, like all church festivals, is poignant with what has gone and eloquent on what we still possess. We scratch around for what is relevant for us in the familiar hymns and readings. We are both glad and a bit uneasy. The attendance is nothing like it once was, perhaps because so many villagers now have no sense of its relevance. The nearest they come to 'harvest' is when they buy an organic loaf. What they actually revere are the tools of the old harvests, the vehicles, the barns, the implements, the collectables. What worries them is the danger lurking in the food chain.

In this respect harvest festival can be a secret statement on the right or traditional use of the land.

The farm has been the centre of invention and improvement for ages. As for the Church, it is notorious for not leaving well alone and, far from being fixed like a star, is always keeping up with the times. Thus harvest festival cannot just be saying old, finished things. When we come to church at Wormingford we see all around us the symbols of what sustains the body and the symbols of what feeds the spirit. They are our basic reminders of what we must have in order to live. The produce of our few farms is that of the present, the Now, to remind us of Christ's insistence that we should neither look back nor forward but exist fully in the moment. 'Having put your hand to the plough, don't look back!' Ploughmen who did not keep on the mark straight ahead – our old ploughmen used a holly-bush in the hedge – ploughed a crooked furrow. The Lord's disciples complained about his brusque dismissal of the past. Did they not have ancestors, customs and all manner of good things in their history? Were they to be abandoned? Of course not, said the Master. They are to be brought into your present. As for the future, well his advice on this would not suit us.

The origin of the word 'harvest' is obscure. It winds in and out of several languages. We come closest to it when we say that we crop what was rooted. The poets like to call this rooting-cropping sequence the everlasting circle. Human existence must go round with this circle whatever age it is in which we live. There are Neolithic burial circles along our river and they make our Wormingford farming seem a very modern business, even when we were doing it in King Alfred's time. Harvest festival has to be a double celebration of field crops and of ourselves as a crop. Moses called it 'the pilgrim feast of ingathering'. Maybe this is what we should dwell on today, the pilgrim feast of ingathering. Robert Hawker of Morwenstowe was the inventor of harvest festival as we know it. His wild parishioners had to be weaned from the dreadful harvest which they gleaned from the sea, the possessions from the ships they wrecked. Weaned too from the goings-on in the barn after they had cut the thin headland corn. So he brought the harvest into the parish church and all the world followed. It is this Victorian harvest festival which we emulate and keep up. 'We plough the fields and scatter . . .' When did we? An old man when I was a boy had done it when he was a boy. It was in a Suffolk village called Boulge, where Edward FitzGerald may have seen him as he translated Omar Khayyam.

Cities

One of my favourite religious broadcasters is Richard Harries, the Bishop of Oxford. I suppose I am prejudiced in his favour because he has what writers recognize as a 'literary intelligence' which draws on novels and poetry. Why, he once asked, are we bound for the *city* of God, rather than the countryside of God? A good question for an age which reveres the village more than it does the town. Yet, why have great Christian writers like St Augustine and John Bunyan mapped our way to the *city* of God? Why in Revelation does St John exercise all his descriptive power to show heaven as a glittering city with golden gates and glassy streets, and not, say, as a meadow in an everlasting springtime, with golden buttercups and skylarks? Or as golden cornfields, for that matter? Right at the very end of the New Testament, almost its last words, we have these words: 'I saw the holy city, New Jerusalem, coming down out of heaven like a bride adorned for her husband . . . Behold, I make all things new.' And it is because of this renewal of the city ideal that we have New York, which was New Amsterdam, New Orleans and then, stretching it a bit, New England and New Zealand. For our ancestors rejected old cities and countries, finding them worn out and oppressive, unjust and corrupt, to sail away to found New Jerusalems, or redeemed versions of their home town. I used to think that they hadn't the wit to think of new names for their new settlements but the reason for making old names new was, of course, theological.

To understand their thinking we have to understand what a city meant to them. We are so used to preferring the country to the streets that we cannot imagine a time when it was the other way round. When it was the country that was uncivilized and the city was 'civil', the centre of art and the law, and all things noble. Man's ultimate social achievement, in fact. When Bunyan was alive you had to get official permission to live in Bedford, his city. It was minute, no more than two thousand or so citizens, but all of them conscious, like St Paul, of belonging to no mean city. Vast human warrens like Tokyo, Los Angeles or London were then unimaginable, and had they existed when Augustine or Bunyan did, I doubt very much if they would have made their heavens such places. Jesus witnessed the new Jerusalem of Herod the Great, a rebuilding which was as much political as religious, and he angered people by recommending them to put their trust in a city not made with hands, and correctly prophesying the destruction of the lovely new Temple in the construction of which Herod aimed to equal King Solomon. Tears filled Christ's eyes as he foresaw the ruin of both his people and their capital, and the sacking and destruction of glorious cities throughout history, Constantinople, Dresden, the City of London, is uniquely heartbreaking.

The most striking thing about St John's New Jerusalem is that it does not have a temple, or in our terms a cathedral, and why? 'And I saw no temple therein, for the Lord God Almighty and the Lamb are its temple.' The Father and his son Christ the King are seated on a throne from which pours the pure water of life itself. Everything about this marvellous city, poetically constructed from glass and gold and jewels, and which stands four-square with guards of angels at its twelve gates is about life. It has a book of life, a river of life and a tree of life. It *lives*.

Human cities live too, though briefly. Even Ur. I love their living splendour. The beauty of earthly cities causes us, like Wordsworth early in the morning on London Bridge, to catch our breath. Venice, Oxford from the surrounding hills, Edinburgh from Arthur's Seat, Istanbul from the river, Sydney from the harbour, or Durham from the train, how they live! Their 'jewels' are usually their temples, plus now the glassy towers of commerce glittering in the rain. St Paul enjoyed a dual citizenship but was proudest of being a Roman. How he respected Rome, only to discover how little it respected him. Yet it was to the Romans that he wrote the superb letter from which every Christian from his day to ours has been taught the social behaviour which causes them to be distinctive. We translate his 'I am a citizen of no mean city' both to heaven and to our local town. For even if we live in the country there is always a town or city to support our rurality. And thus we too have a double allegiance, to the country parish and to where the library, supermarket, college, cathedral, theatre, etc., are.

Jesus had the great tragedy of not being welcome in his home town Nazareth. Daring to criticize its religious attitudes he barely escaped with his life. So where to now? Not far away was the Roman garrison city Capernaum, and he used it as his base. The synagogue there was a gift by an army officer to the strange people he was stationed among. If it was the one in which Jesus sometimes preached and taught, often dissentingly, we do not hear that he was ever asked to leave, as he had been at Nazareth, where he said, 'A prophet is not without honour except in his own country.' His kingdom has no capital city. There is nothing there other than 'my Father's house', which is our final abiding place, and where there is room for us all. That 'Abide with us, for it is toward evening, and the day is far spent' at the end of the Emmaus road will be the 'Abide with me' invitation when we come to the end of our journey.

Tramping from city to city across the Roman empire, having to identify himself frequently when challenged '*Quo vadis*?', St Paul's letters are filled with military language. He tells the Church that it is a power within a power – 'For we wrestle not against flesh and blood, but against the rulers of the darkness of this world, and against spiritual wickedness in high places.' Nero reigned. Hitler would reign. Paul tells Christians to be like a spiritual version of the strength which they saw every day, that of a regiment, a centurion, a brave defender of a city. 'Take unto you the whole armour of God, that you may be able to withstand the evil day. Have your loins girt about with truth' – Roman soldiers wore a low-slung belt – 'and put on the breastplate of righteousness, and your feet shod with the preparation of the gospel of peace.' Paul is the quartermaster fitting out the Lord's own force, with 'the shield of faith' and 'the helmet of salvation'. His marching orders arrive from Rome itself to the city of Ephesus. Not only are Christ's followers there to fight in his cause but they are to turn themselves into spiritual building blocks to make 'a holy temple in the Lord' which has to challenge that of the goddess Diana.

William Blake's 'Jerusalem' continues St Paul's metaphor of the soldier-architect, of the city defender, the city-maker.

> Bring me my bow of burning gold!
>   Bring me my arrows of desire!
> Bring me my spear! O clouds, unfold!
>   Bring me my chariot of fire!
> I will not cease from mental fight,
>   Nor shall my sword sleep in my hand,
> Till we have built Jerusalem
>   In England's green and pleasant land.

Blake lived in the West End of London, a huge city which was dirty, grand, immensely rich, dreadfully poor, heartless, filled with innumerable kindnesses and cruelties, noisy, noble, terrible, all the things which a city is. He also lived for a spell in the country and found it no better.

As I Was Saying . . .

W hen we think of the Bible we are inclined to believe that its messages, commands, laws and insights all come to us via official statements, whereas many of its great teachings reach us via talk – via conversation.

In the Bible there is preaching and there is talking, and most of its great figures are heard doing both. The Lord preached a long sermon on a piece of raised ground – the first and best of all Christian sermons. It is profound and wonderfully beautiful. After the Sermon on the Mount all other Christian sermons are really superfluous. It is all there, the gospel, the sense, the glory. And there were other occasions when he looked around for a natural pulpit on the ground, or on a ship, or in the Temple, sometimes to preach, sometimes to tell stories. His preaching could be learned or alarmingly simple. He called his stories parables or putting things side by side. They were a way of removing the barrier. The form was an ancient one and when the crowd heard the opening sentence – 'There was once a rich man who dressed in purple and the finest linen' . . . 'There was a rich man who had a steward' . . . 'There was a poor man . . .' – it would have been riveted.

And yet frequently, far more so than we realize, Jesus spoke without preaching, without climbing up to the raised place. He simply talked. He would get into conversation with an individual with no thought for whether it was male or female. Often it was to help a person discover himself and to know how to talk to God. This casual conversation of his could lead him into danger. People with closed minds are troubled by free speech. The country was occupied by foreigners and his own religion was in the hands of those who dreaded any rocking of the boat, any keen controversy. And here was a young rabbi who could get them all arrested – who could get the new Temple flattened and who, worst of all, showed them up as bigots. The ultra-right Pharisees thought they must put a stop to it before it got out of hand, this preaching the kingdom, this stirring-up version of the faith. Thus, in Matthew's words, they thought 'how they might entangle him in his talk'. Unfortunately for their plan, they forgot that this disturber of the peace was a master of language and that the kind of kingdom which they had in mind meant nothing to him. All the same, they tried to entangle him in his talk, the usual lawyer's tactic.

They begin with flattery. 'We know you are brave and true, not giving a fig for what the world is saying about you, *but tell us where you stand*. What are your politics? Do *you* think it right that we should have to pay a levy to Rome?'

Equally conversationally, Jesus says, 'Show me tribute

money.' And they give him a penny stamped with the head of Tiberias.

He holds it up. 'Whose head and name is on this coin?'

'Caesar's!'

'Then give to Caesar the things that are Caesar's, and to God the things that are God's.'

We recognize from the trip-up questions of our own times a chill undercurrent in this conversation. It anticipates the trial in the judgement hall. For a second or two Christ has been put in the dock, the place of entangling talk. One unwise word and they could have had him for sedition.

St Paul loved conversation. He was for ever telling his converts to converse and was severe with the Philippian church – Philippi was where the gospel was first preached beyond Palestine – ordering his friends there to 'elevate' their conversation, 'be as becometh the gospel of Christ'. Their talk was not always to be about materialism – 'We should leave such talk to those whose God is their belly. *Our* conversation is in heaven, where we look for the Saviour.' What does Paul mean – 'Our conversation is in heaven'? He means that it should be fit for their Lord to hear, that it should be uplifting, though conversation all the same. Writing to young Timothy, his able, loyal helper, Paul tells him, 'Let no man despise your youth. Be an example of what a Christian should be, in word, in conversation, in love, in spirit, in faith, in purity. Read and study, and don't neglect the gifts which God has given you. Meditate, and show the kind of young man you are by the way in which you *talk*.'

Every kind of statistic exists for our lives. They tell us that we spend a third of them asleep, several years of them eating, ages dressing, a week shaving, vast chunks of them toiling and, should you be English, an unbelievable time gardening – and now a shocking amount of time shopping and watching television. But there is no statistic for the time we spend in conversation, no figure for one of the most pleasant and compulsive human activities. In Peter's first Letter there is the remarkable statement that men are frequently brought to Christ by 'the conversation, or conduct of their wives', something which reminds us of the power of women in the early Church.

Among the most terrible of fates is to be deprived of conversation – to be cut off from ordinary talk. Countless prisoners have suffered – and suffer – this. Robinson Crusoe suffered it most of all on his island, Elementary talk with Man Friday was no compensation because, being a 'savage' he was not yet a 'man', for this is how native peoples were often regarded in the 18th century. Old people say that they would sooner sometimes have a nice conversation than a meal on wheels. We come to church to pray and listen and sing – and to have a word with old friends we won't see again until next Sunday.

Talking to each other can be a way of talking to God.

Jesus's conversational voice is heard along the road to Emmaus, intimate, directed to those who keep step with him.

The Sayings of Jesus

---◆---

I have been given a little book entitled *The Sayings of Jesus* in which the commands, the conversations, the prayers and the teachings of Christ have been extracted from the four Gospels so as to give their very pith and essence. Nearly all the sayings are familiar, of course, and yet at the same time they now seem to possess an added force because of their not being surrounded by story and sermon. Here in about fifty pages are the heart and soul of the Lord. This book is the work of Andrew Lindzey who until recently taught at the Theology Centre of Essex University, a remarkable place, very vital and interesting. I heard Archbishop Desmond Tutu there, Dr Runcie and the Bishop of Durham. They spoke to enormous audiences, and each of them in his own way lived by the sayings of Jesus.

How did these life-giving sayings survive the years between their being uttered and their being written down? By being remembered by those who had actually heard Jesus speak. There is no reference to notes being taken even when he sometimes taught a class like a rabbi. The only scribes present were those sent by the authorities to record, hopefully, criticism of the government, for it had become urgent to put an end to this popular teacher's dangerous statements. This soon proved impossible. When he returned to the Father who was the source and inspiration of this new language, they soon found out that although the great teacher had left no records to be censored, everything he had said was safely locked in the hearts and heads of his followers. These men and women, and surely some children, were at first devastated by his absence and hardly knew where to turn or what to do. Then they discovered that repeating something which they had heard him speak brought him back to them as powerfully as when he stopped walking and began talking, only differently.

What happened was that the affectionate recalling of Jesus in both word and deed – for had he not told them over and over again how futile it was to talk and not act? – brought both the master and themselves to Life with a capital L. His original words continued to fill not only the air but the entire universe. What had been said could never be unsaid. If a mere official, Pilate, saw that there was no going back on one's word – 'What I have written I have written' – what hope was there of rubbing out words which started as unwritten law? Simply remembering them was death-defeating. They were never in the past tense and were new every day. People told themselves that it was not what he *had* said but what he was saying that very morning, that very night. The Gospels acquired their authority and beauty because Jesus talks, rather than talked, on the page.

He was keen on memory as a revitalizing agent of the present, and was never what we call nostalgic. Why did he say, 'Do this in remembrance of me every time you come to the fellowship of a meal?' Why did he say, 'Remember Lot's wife?' (Don't look back, look ahead, is what he is saying here.) Most of all, why did he wrap his message up in short stories? Well, what is more memorable than a good short story? – and the Lord's were unforgettable. If one may be allowed to be childish, they acted like jam concealing a pill which the untheological listener would otherwise find hard to swallow. We can well imagine a mother or father coming home with a first-hand story from Jesus, retelling it at bedtime to their children, and they, eventually, telling it to their children. For stories are for the retelling.

Jesus leaves the listener with a nerve-racking amount of choice. 'If anyone hears my sayings and does not keep them, I do not judge him. For I did not come to judge the world but to save it. He who rejects me and does not receive my sayings has a judge.' We have received his sayings, first because those who heard them could not forget them, and then because when they were threatened by natural forgetfulness, someone wrote them down.

We now rely not only on the permanence of the printed page, but on film footage and tapes. The other day I listened to myself and the artist John Nash having a talk by the fireside thirty years ago. It was strangely moving to hear the logs crackling and the clock ticking. But little of what I have heard others say during my life is on tape and the essence of their personalities is often concentrated in a saying or two. I remember a saying of my mother's when we children were chattering away and holding up the meal by forgetting to eat. 'Whistle and ride!' she would say. Her mother must have said that. And a friend's mother is encapsulated in something she always said when she read the paper and saw all the wars and crimes – 'Oh, Jim, I do wish they wouldn't!'

The sayings of Jesus cover every human experience, some grand and cosmic, many gentle and intimate. They remind us that he is both our King and our close friend. He rules, he loves, he guides. He is enthroned – though sometimes in one of our chairs. Those quiet, meant-only-for-your-ears sayings of his remind us of the intimacy of God. 'As the Father has loved me, so have I loved you.'

Life is fraught and uncertain, as the collect reminds us: 'O God, who knowest us to be set in the midst of so many and great dangers, that by reason of the frailty of our nature we cannot always stand upright, grant us such strength and protection as may support us.' The sayings of Jesus are uniquely supportive. He too showed human frailty. He too was over-worked and weary. He too lost those nearest to him. He's seen it all, as we would say. And so he says, 'Don't try to be self-sufficient.' He says, 'Do not be excessively con-cerned about food or clothes or drink or money or pos-ition.' He harks on the brevity of human life and the way it is wasted by obsession and materialism. Reading the sayings of Jesus collectively shows how balanced they are, how proportionate to our needs. In St Mark's Gospel he says, 'Take heed what you hear; the measure you give will be the measure you get.'

His first recorded sayings were in his own church and the congregation was enchanted. Nazareth had no reputation for prophetic eloquence, as we know. 'Did any man speak like this?' But when, later, he touched them on the raw they could not take it, and they ran him out of town. Later, too, the authorities recognized that they were having to confront a master of debate and they sought 'how to entangle him in his language' by the usual legal trickery – how to bring him down. It proved impossible. They actually found him hard to understand in ordinary religious and moral terms, and they once asked him, 'Where do you stand? What are your politics? Who is your God?' And when he told them they shuddered.

Remembering and acting upon the sayings of Jesus goes on being a formative experience. They are proof of the huge truth of John 6: 'The words I have spoken to you are both spirit and life.'

'Time Is Man's Angel'

'*Time is man's angel*'

(Schiller *The Death of Wallenstein* 1798)

Religion places time and timelessness together – places them in parallel. Not that they can stay together for very long. Our time runs out, our timelessness runs nowhere, for that is its property. It just is. When God became man in order to enter what he had created, being now human, he experienced time. The Incarnation was God's experience of being born, growing up, becoming native to a particular country, being loved by a particular family, becoming a teacher and spiritual healer who challenged local laws and customs, and having to endure the local justice. All this within the bounds of time. The Gospels are most careful to state when and where Jesus was in time. 'Now when Jesus was born in Bethlehem of Judaea in the days of Herod the king . . .' 'And it came to pass in those days that there went out a decree from Caesar Augustus that all the world should be taxed, and this taxing was first made when Cyrenius was governor of Syria . . .' The historical Jesus, as the biographers call him, is set fairly and clearly within his times, just as each one of us is, courtesy of our birth certificates, bank accounts, national health cards and passports. Not to mention the Baptism register. Here we are, on the earth, fully documented and date-stamped all over.

Whilst here on the earth, Jesus showed scant respect for time. He criticized those who allowed it to dominate their lives in such a way that they 'hadn't the time to take their time', as the playright Ionesco put it. Not to have a spare minute, let alone a spare hour, is a cause of bragging in our village. Congratulate me, the incessantly busy are asking when they tell us, 'I never have a minute to myself', 'I don't have time to turn round,' 'I just managed to get everything done in time'.

Time is at its grandest, at its most awe-inspiring, in the Bible. First, from the Letter to the Hebrews, consider that glorious opening chapter which begins, 'God, who at sundry times and in divers manners spake in time past unto the fathers by the prophets, hath in these last days spoken unto us by his Son . . .' And then the even more stupendous opening of St John's Gospel – 'In the beginning was the Word.' Both writers run time and timelessness, mortality and immortality, the temporal and the eternal, side by side like twin tracks on a railway line, one going as far as the terminus, the other out of sight. The Incarnate One arrived at a moment when it became agonizingly plain to him that his earthly existence was over, although it was not this which brought that 'It is finished' to his lips but the realization that he had completed the task his Father had set for him. What was finished was his work on earth and also his life in time. 'I completed it.' The redemption we call it, this divine work. To redeem means to buy back, usually at a high price. We have been repossessed by God and now we can take our place at the table of his family, the Church, where although the old tower clock clunks and chimes its way through the service, there is no set time. We have stepped into the immeasurable, into that time for everything which the Bible calls 'rest'.

We have nailed mortal time down to the split second, to the carbon-tested age of a tree-stump put down as a marker in what is now Norfolk which was growing when Abraham pitched his tent at Bethel, and to an exactitude which previous generations would have found a burden. For them it was daybreak or noon or evening or night. It was spring or it was summer or autumn or winter. It was the Feast of St Peter or St Petronilla, Christmas (all twelve days), or maybe one's own birthday, although one could never be quite sure. And so life went on, *sans* minutes and hours for the most part. The sun came up and the sun went down. The tides went out and the tides came in. The birds flew away, only God knew where, and the birds flew home, joy, joy. The Lord would come in his own good time, though please God not yet. Ditto Father Time. Then a great gold clock was fixed on the parish church and its hands told every hand when to start and when to stop, and Time ruled the roost.

The Preacher of Ecclesiastes offers a philosophy of Time –

the best there is. He is among other things the master of weariness, of disillusionment. He has done it all, seen it all, had it all. His Time is quite unlike that of medieval Christians, which pounced on them when they were dancing or making love or gathering flowers, suddenly bringing them down like 'the Fallen' in modern wars. The Preacher allows time for everything, but it is an allowance. There follows, logically, a time to cease doing this, or being that, sad though it is. And reading his beautiful statement, we have to agree. There *is* a time to weep and a time to laugh, a time to embrace and a time to refrain from embracing, a time to keep silence and a time to speak, a time to be born and a time to die. There is in a lifetime a time for everything once we have learned how to find the time. That is the secret.

Wiltshire Rickyard

On Not Paying Attention

I have often thought that an interesting book could be written on what happens to children during a church service, both historically and currently. Adults allow that they must be bored or puzzled or restless or even a nuisance, but not that they may not be any of these things. Grown up, we forget the behaviour that adults expected of us during a service and remember things which they would not have seen or heard due to their having belonged to our daydream. It is the prerogative of children to daydream in class or pew, or at plays or concerts to which we are taken for our good. I have watched a child at church full of attention, but not for anything I am saying. Daydreams are set off by the imagination being awakened by a private interpretation of an interior, let's say, or the way the candles leap in the draught, or a stone face looking down, or some strangely beautiful words which are incomprehensible. Make the most of this state, advised Wordsworth, for it will fade with maturity. Except for artists, poets and a few saints, and the not quite sane, the best daydreaming is probably over as soon as one starts to pay attention.

I was a notoriously inattentive child in church. What was

more, I knew how to put on a semblance of keen interest in what was officially happening so as never to get a nudge or a 'Sit up straight!' I could look to left and right without turning my head and take in wondrous tombs and rows of singing mouths in profile, and could look up without looking away from the pulpit and dote on the angels in the roof. He is so good in church, they said, a model child worshipper. Although you did occasionally have to give him a look when he was turning his Bible round to read the maps. William Morris is reputed to have had his entire life changed by a revelation he had in Canterbury Cathedral, which was that everything he saw had been hand-made. He was a boy exercising his prerogative to daydream in high places. As his gaze wandered it came to him in a Pauline flash that what poured from the post-industrial revolution factory could never compete with what issued from the craftsman's workshop. Though perhaps there is too much utility in this tale for it to be qualified as a daydream. Church daydreams do not support theology or archaeology. They bypass the rector's glance and have a territory behind the hymns and liturgy where they can do absolutely what they like, whatever they have a mind to.

The trouble is that an ancient aisle is so fascinating. Will this be the morning when the arches fall? The Second Coming created a special reverie – mostly about the logistics of lifting the roof. Trapped birds and butterflies, and once a dragonfly from the Stour just outside zigzagging close enough to the wide summer door for it to escape, which it could not, would preoccupy me. Eventually tremendous praying on my part caused it to zig out to the river. I went with it, leaving my body in the church as cover for my dream flight. Thomas Hardy could not keep out of church from infancy to old age. He would bike several miles on a Sunday to read the lesson for a friend, perhaps one of his favourites from the Books of Kings. The Rationalists had a good mind to blackball him because he would go to church. His was the most marvellous church daydream of all for, being a poet, he did not have to terminate it at puberty. Stinsford Church contained most of the dramatis personae he would require later on. The handsome memorial to a young man named Angel must often have distracted his gaze from the Tate and Brady page.

We had hissing gaslight for Evensong which provided me with a curious notion of the Pentecostal Spirit as I watched the nervous jab of the flames in their half-frosted globes. Winter Evensong in St Peter's, Sudbury, with the bells crashing above the statue to Thomas Gainsborough and, inside, the huge rich Tractarian reredos glimmering in the painted chancel, and the snowy choir sweeping in like an advertisement for washday, and the identical Misses Willet, dressmakers, in their pew, and Canon Hughes rocking along towards his stall, his pate like that of a Desert Father, soaring and creamy – here was a world in which a child's imagination might tour for ever, it seemed. It was better than the pictures, and Mr Vinnicombe's recessional splendours on the starry organ – it was powered by water, which made it the more magical – would come all too soon. William Cowper mourned his passing 'From reveries so airy' to the toil

> Of dropping buckets into empty wells,
> And growing old in drawing nothing up.

Not, I hasten to reassure myself, that it has come to that. Having been allowed (nobody appeared to notice) much uninterrupted musing on anything other than the sermon, and much speculation on the extraordinary objects and sounds which furnish the Church of England, and many flights of history, and carefree views of salvation, I fear that I have not quite put away childish things and can still dream through part of our village worship. I am much attached to the butterfly colours which the east window at Mount Bures throws on Mr Gurdon's tablet, and I have to avoid looking at it if I need another kind of concentration – on what I am about to say, for example. That church is dedicated to St John the Baptist whose day falls on the summer solstice, when the old people who dreamed their religion away on our local hill thought that the sun paused. I expect there were solstitial fires up there before he arrived and boys and girls would go home with the bonfire blazing in their heads to dream wonders which put them at a loss for words.

I suppose that for some religious their Rule is a kind of

organized day and night dreaming, of reverie by the clock. But if I get too engrossed in my own thoughts when I'm supposed to be leading the service, I hear Benedict's cry of 'Discipline!' in my free-ranging ear. Or I wake up to hear half the congregation murmuring, 'You forgot the psalm!' I would not leave out the psalm for anything. It just goes to prove the evils of not concentrating, of letting the imagination off the leash, of being ten all over again.

ACKNOWLEDGEMENTS AND BIBLIOGRAPHY

Appleton, George, *Jerusalem Prayers for the World Today*.

Bible, Authorized Version and New English.

Book of Common Prayer.

Blythe, Ronald, *Divine Landscapes*, Viking, 1986, Canterbury Press Norwich, 1998.

Blythe, Ronald, *All This Blessedness is Ours*, Julian Lectures, 1995.

Blythe, Ronald, *Talking About John Clare*, Nottingham-Trent University, 2000.

Causley, Charles, 'Coming from Evening Church', *Collected Poems* © Macmillan, 1990, permission sought.

Cohn-Sherbok, Dan, *The Sayings of Moses*, Duckworth, 1991.

Hopkins, Gerard Manley, *Collected Poems*.

Hymns Ancient and Modern, Canterbury Press Norwich, 1922, 1950 and 1983.

Julian of Norwich, *Revelations of Divine Love*, translated by Clifton Wolters, Penguin, 1966.

Linzey, Andrew, *The Sayings of Jesus*, Duckworth, 1991.

New English Hymnal, Canterbury Press Norwich, 1986.

Ramsey, Michael, *Be Still and Know*, Fount, 1982.

Rolle, Richard, *The Fire of Love*, translated by Clifton Wolters, Penguin, 1981.

Saint John of the Cross, *Poems*, translated by Roy Campbell, Harvill Press, 1952.

Staniforth, Maxwell, *Early Christian Writings: The Apostolic Fathers*, Penguin, 1982.

Thomas, Dylan, 'And death shall have no dominion', *Collected Poems 1934–52*, © Dent, 1952, permission sought.

Traherne, Thomas, *Centuries*, Oxford University Press.

Robin Tanner's etchings on pages xiv, 13, 29, 67, 93, 145, 173 and 197 are taken from *Robin Tanner: The Etchings* published by Garton & Co., 1988, permission sought. The etching on page 127 is taken from Heather and Robin Tanner, *A Country Book of Days* published by Old Style Press, 1986, permission sought. All etchings are © the Estate of Robin Tanner.